make it DISCARD in minutes

easy recipes in 15 20 & 30 minutes

Wiley Publishing, Inc.

A Word About Weight Watchers

Since 1963, Weight Watchers has grown from a handful of people to millions of enrollments annually. Today, Weight Watchers is recognized as the leading name in safe and sensible weight control. Weight Watchers members form diverse groups, from youths to senior citizens, attending meetings virtually around the globe. Weight loss and weight management results vary by individual, but we recommend that you attend Weight Watchers meetings, follow the Weight Watchers food plan, and participate in regular physical activity. For the Weight Watchers meeting nearest you, call 800-651-6000.

Also, visit us at our Web site:
www.weightwatchers.com

Weight Watchers Publishing Group

Creative and Editorial Director:
 Nancy Gagliardi

Editorial Assistant: Jenny Laboy-Brace

Recipe Editors: Kevin Morrissey,
 Eileen Runyan

Recipe Developers: David Bonom,
 Maureen Luchejko

Photography: Ann Stratton

Food Styling: Anne Disrude

Prop Styling: Betty Alfenito

Wiley Publishing, Inc.

Executive Editor: Anne Ficklen

Production Editor: Helen Chin

Cover Design: Edwin Kuo

Interior Design: Edwin Kuo and Sue Irish

Page Layout: Nick Anderson

Manufacturing Buyer: Kevin Watt

For general information on our other products and services or to obtain technical support please contact our Customer Care Department within the U.S. at 800-762-2974, outside the U.S. at 317-572-3993 or fax 317-572-4002.

Wiley also publishes its books in a variety of electronic formats. Some content that appears in print may not be available in electronic books.

Library of Congress Cataloging-in-Publication Data

Weight Watchers make it in minutes : easy recipes in 15, 20, and 30 minutes.
    p. cm.
  Includes index.
  ISBN 0-7645-6517-6 (paperback : alk. paper)
  1. Reducing diets—Recipes. 2. Quick and easy cookery. I. Title: Make it in minutes.
  II. Weight Watchers International
RM222.2 . W32114 2001
641.5'635—dc21   2001039156

FRONT COVER PHOTO: Sesame-Glazed Shrimp with Snow Peas and Baby Corn (page 132)
BACK COVER PHOTOS (LEFT TO RIGHT): Maple-Berry Pancakes (page 154);
  Farfalle Bolognese (page 220); Polynesian Pineapple Chicken (page 58)

Manufactured in the United States of America
10 9 8 7 6

Table of Contents

Introduction

Several years ago, we here at the Weight Watchers Publishing Group created a Special Interest Publication (SIP), a fancy name used by people in the publishing world for a bigger, glossier version of a traditional magazine that was available exclusively in Weight Watchers meetings rooms. Called *In a Flash*, this spectacular, yet slim, volume of over 100 recipes made a big promise: breakfasts, lunches, and dinners in 15, 20, and 30 minutes. We went to our best recipe developers, asking them not only to come up with dishes that lived up to the Weight Watchers reputation—that is, they had to taste absolutely delicious—but also to really deliver on the time promise.

We soon found out that people really used the SIP, that the recipes lived up to their speedy promise, and that they tasted terrific. Clearly, this was a topic—and a format—that people wanted and, more importantly, truly needed. As an editor who works on creating several cookbooks per year, nothing pleases me more than knowing that the information and recipes we're providing are actually being used, as well as helping people to reach their goals.

So the SIP, now out of print, led us to *Make It in Minutes*. This brand new book keeps the original promises so popular with our members, and expands them for both Weight Watchers members and the general public. In other words, whether you're a current, former, or never Weight Watchers member and interested in cooking—and eating—healthy food, *Make It in Minutes* has 200 tempting, clearly organized recipes for breakfast, lunch, and dinner.

If you thought you were too busy to cook healthy food or start a healthy food plan because it seemed like too much work, the newly developed recipes we created exclusively for *Make It in Minutes* will banish those excuses. In fact, with *Make It in Minutes* you'll find the answers to all your mealtime questions. We've provided delicious ideas for breakfast and lunch, as well as dinner. (We think brown-baggers especially will appreciate the great recipes we've developed to spice up their midday meals.) These recipes also work for everyday family meals as well as entertaining; we're sure that they will become staples that you use over and over again.

We also know that it can be a challenge deciding on what to serve to round out your meal, so we've added a special feature to the recipes called "What's for Dinner" (or Lunch or Breakfast, as the case may be). These inventive ideas require little or no cooking, yet keep you safely on the path of healthy eating, no matter how harried your life may be.

The success of *In a Flash* lets us know that *Make It in Minutes* will be a must-have cookbook for busy cooks everywhere. It's a great example of how the right idea will just keep on growing, until it reaches as many people as possible.

Nancy Gagliardi
Creative & Editorial Director

minute recipes

DINNER

Coffee Yogurt and Cookie Parfait

Makes 2 servings

4 anisette toasts, broken into bite-size pieces

1 (8-ounce) container nonfat coffee yogurt

$1/2$ cup light nondairy whipped topping

Give someone special a romantic breakfast treat with Italian flair. The recipe easily doubles or triples. The licorice flavor of the toasts complements the coffee yogurt making the combination reminiscent of a mellow, Sambuca-spiked coffee. Look for the crunchy anisette toasts in the cookie or Italian aisle of your supermarket, or in a grocery store specializing in Italian products.

Put $1/4$ cup of the toast pieces into the bottom of each glass. Layer with $1/4$ cup yogurt, 2 tablespoons whipped topping, another $1/4$ cup of the toast pieces, and another $1/4$ cup yogurt. Top each with another 2 tablespoons whipped topping.

What's for Breakfast

Sliced fresh strawberries, mango, or papaya add a touch of the exotic to this refreshing, sweet morning treat.

COOK'S TIP   To serve as an elegant dessert, layer the parfait in large wine goblets and decorate with a few shavings of good quality chocolate.

3 POINTS per serving

Per serving:
163 Calories • 1 g Total Fat • 0 g Saturated Fat • 25 mg Cholesterol • 173 mg Sodium • 32 g Total Carbohydrate
0 g Dietary Fiber • 5 g Protein • 147 mg Calcium

Tropical Yogurt Cooler

Juicy tropical fruit adds flavor to this frosty yogurt drink. It's an intensely cooling drink, a perfect breakfast for a steamy summer day. For an even richer drink, add one tablespoon malted-milk powder to the mixture.

*Makes 2 servings
(yield 2 cups)*

1 ripe mango, peeled and cut into chunks (about 1 cup)

1 ripe papaya, peeled, seeded, and cut into chunks (about 1 cup)

1/2 cup plain nonfat yogurt

2 tablespoons honey

1 teaspoon fresh lime juice

6 ice cubes

Puree the mango, papaya, yogurt, honey, lime juice, and ice in a blender.

What's for Breakfast

This drink makes a refreshing accompaniment to toasted, frozen waffles. Pack them for a breakfast-on-the-run or for an in-the-office breakfast.

COOK'S TIP Use precut fruit from your local supermarket's produce section or salad bar for an even speedier splash.

4 POINTS per serving

Per serving:
225 Calories • 1 g Total Fat • 0 g Saturated Fat • 1 mg Cholesterol • 54 mg Sodium • 55 g Total Carbohydrate
5 g Dietary Fiber • 5 g Protein • 170 mg Calcium

Chocolate-Raspberry Frosty

Neither kids nor grownups will ever tire of the endless possible variations of this thick chocolaty treat. One day use raspberries, the next strawberries, and the next bananas. You could even add canned apricots to the frozen yogurt mix; just be sure to drain them well first.

*Makes 4 servings
(yield 2¹/₂ cups)*

1 pint chocolate nonfat frozen yogurt

¹/₂ cup low-fat (1%) milk

¹/₂ cup fresh, or thawed frozen, raspberries

2 tablespoons raspberry syrup

Puree the frozen yogurt, milk, raspberries, and syrup in a blender.

What's for Breakfast

The chewy texture of a favorite low-fat granola bar will contrast well with this smooth cool drink.

Per serving (generous ¹/₂ cup):
132 Calories • 0 g Total Fat • 0 g Saturated Fat • 1 mg Cholesterol • 90 mg Sodium • 28 g Total Carbohydrate
2 g Dietary Fiber • 4 g Protein • 491 mg Calcium

2 POINTS per serving

Coconut-Pineapple Smoothie

The California coolers called smoothies are refreshing, thirst-quenching, and free of all the additives typically found in soft drinks They are popular for breakfast, but for a satisfying mid-afternoon snack, treat yourself to a macaroon or sugar wafer along with this delightful drink.

Makes 2 servings

¹/₂ pint coconut sorbet, softened

¹/₂ cup crushed pineapple in juice, drained

¹/₄ cup unsweetened pineapple juice

¹/₄ cup orange juice

1 small banana, sliced

1 teaspoon coconut extract

Puree the sorbet, pineapple, pineapple juice, orange juice, banana, and coconut extract in a blender. Serve in tall glasses.

What's for Breakfast

Try this tropical teaser with a few chunks of fresh kiwi fruit, mango, or papaya, placed in the bottom of the glass and a slice of sweet brioche on the side.

 COOK'S TIP To soften frozen sorbet, pop it in the refrigerator 15 minutes before using.

4 POINTS per serving

Per serving:
216 Calories • 0 g Total Fat • 0 g Saturated Fat • 0 mg Cholesterol • 32 mg Sodium • 52 g Total Carbohydrate
2 g Dietary Fiber • 1 g Protein • 20 mg Calcium

Fruit with Cannoli Cream

This quick and easy treat fit for family or company, makes the most of the array of precut fresh fruit now available at your local supermarket. Stop by the salad bar on your way home from work and have a delicious breakfast the next morning.

Makes 3 servings

3 cups mixed fruit (such as sliced strawberries, blueberries, melon cubes, or grapes)

3 tablespoons orange juice

$1^1/_2$ tablespoons chopped fresh mint

$^1/_4$ cup part-skim ricotta cheese

$1^1/_2$ tablespoons confectioners' sugar

$^1/_8$ teaspoon vanilla extract

1 Combine the fruit, orange juice, and mint and spoon into serving bowls.

2 Puree the ricotta cheese, confectioners' sugar, and vanilla in a blender or food processor. Spoon over the fruit.

What's for Breakfast

This creamy fruit concoction is delicious accompanied by cinnamon toast.

 COOK'S TIP This recipe can do double duty as dessert, too. For a decidedly grown-up flavor, substitute an equal amount of orange liqueur for the juice.

2 POINTS per serving

Per serving:
108 Calories • 2 g Total Fat • 1 g Saturated Fat • 6 mg Cholesterol • 37 mg Sodium • 20 g Total Carbohydrate
3 g Dietary Fiber • 4 g Protein • 76 mg Calcium

Fruity Cottage Cheese Toasts

Kids will absolutely love this tasty, vanilla-and-cinnamon-laced breakfast treat. Another way to enjoy it is to layer the sweetened cottage cheese and fruit in parfait glasses, and top with graham cracker squares.

*Makes 4 servings
(yield 2 cups)*

1 cup fat-free cottage cheese

2 tablespoons confectioners' sugar

1/4 teaspoon vanilla extract

1/4 teaspoon ground cinnamon

1 (15-ounce) can light fruit cocktail, drained

8 slices cinnamon-raisin bread, toasted and cut into triangles

Puree the cottage cheese, confectioners' sugar, vanilla, and cinnamon in a blender or food processor. Transfer the mixture to a bowl and stir in the fruit. Spoon onto the toast triangles.

What's for Breakfast

Serve the toast triangles with fresh-squeezed orange juice.

 For a truly tropical flavor, create your own fruit salad of mango, papaya, pineapple, cantaloupe, and kiwi fruit.

1 POINT per serving

Per serving:
81 Calories • 0 g Total Fat • 0 g Saturated Fat • 2 mg Cholesterol • 11 mg Sodium • 13 g Total Carbohydrate
1 g Dietary Fiber • 6 g Protein • 13 mg Calcium

Orange-Scented French Toast with Fresh Strawberries

Orange zest and orange juice infuse this indulgent breakfast with a fresh citrus accent. For an added treat, mix blueberries and raspberries in with the strawberries.

Makes 2 servings

1 pint strawberries, cleaned and hulled

1^1/$_2$ tablespoons sugar

1 teaspoon grated orange zest

2 large eggs

1 large egg white

^{1}/$_4$ cup fat-free milk

2 tablespoons orange juice

^{1}/$_2$ teaspoon vanilla extract

Pinch ground ginger

4 slices whole-wheat bread

1 Place the strawberries, sugar, and orange zest in a small bowl; mix well.

2 Whisk together the eggs, egg white, milk, orange juice, vanilla, and ginger in a shallow bowl. Add 2 slices of the bread and soak, turning, until saturated, about 1 minute.

3 Spray a large nonstick skillet lightly with nonstick spray. Transfer the bread to the skillet and cook over medium-low heat until nicely browned and puffed, 2–3 minutes on each side. Repeat with the remaining 2 slices bread. Serve with the strawberries.

What's for Breakfast

To finish the French toast with a flourish, drizzle with fruit syrup and serve with a dollop of low-fat vanilla yogurt.

 COOK'S TIP Store berries in their supermarket containers in the refrigerator until you are ready to use them. *Don't* clean them as rinsing will cause them to deteriorate more quickly. Room temperature berries taste better than cold, straight-from-the-refrigerator berries, so for best flavor let the berries come to room temperature for one hour or so before serving.

7 POINTS per serving

Per serving:
328 Calories • 9 g Total Fat • 2 g Saturated Fat • 213 mg Cholesterol • 407 mg Sodium • 50 g Total Carbohydrate
7 g Dietary Fiber • 16 g Protein • 128 mg Calcium

Oatmeal Porridge with Raisins, Apricots, and Figs

Makes 2 servings
(yield 2 cups)

2 cups water

²/3 cup quick-cooking rolled oats

¹/4 cup raisins

¹/4 cup dried apricots, sliced

2 dried figs, quartered

1 tablespoon sugar

¹/2 teaspoon vanilla extract

¹/2 teaspoon ground cinnamon

¹/8 teaspoon ground cardamom

¹/8 teaspoon salt

A generous assortment of fruit makes this a fiber-rich breakfast a welcoming way to start the day, while quick-cooking oatmeal makes preparation a snap. Feel free to substitute your favorite dried fruit, or stir in some fresh fruit just before the porridge is through cooking. Splash with a little fat-free milk, if you like.

Bring the water to a boil in a saucepan. Stir in the oats, raisins, apricots, figs, sugar, vanilla, cinnamon, cardamom, and salt. Bring to a boil, reduce the heat to medium-low and simmer, uncovered, until the liquid is absorbed and the fruit softened, 5–10 minutes.

What's for Breakfast

 Just perfect with a cup of frothy hot chocolate on a wintry morning.

COOK'S TIP Use kitchen scissors to quickly cut the dried fruit.

Per serving:
278 Calories • 2 g Total Fat • 0 g Saturated Fat • 0 mg Cholesterol • 153 mg Sodium • 64 g Total Carbohydrate
6 g Dietary Fiber • 6 g Protein • 65 mg Calcium

5 POINTS per serving

Blueberry-Almond Oatmeal Cream

Start your day with this comforting and energizing oatmeal, dotted with vitamin-rich blueberries. As rich and creamy as rice pudding, it's not only delicious for breakfast, but also as a dessert.

Makes 4 servings
(yield 4 cups)

3 cups water

2 cups quick-cooking rolled oats

1/4 cup packed light brown sugar

1/2 teaspoon ground cinnamon

1/8 teaspoon ground nutmeg

1 1/2 cups light nondairy whipped topping

1 cup fresh, or thawed frozen, blueberries

1/2 cup low-fat (1%) milk

1 tablespoon sliced almonds, toasted

Combine the water, oats, brown sugar, cinnamon, and nutmeg in a saucepan; bring to a boil. Cook, stirring constantly, until the mixture thickens slightly, about 5 minutes. Remove from the heat; fold in the whipped topping, blueberries, and milk. Sprinkle with the almonds before serving.

What's for Breakfast

 Perfect with a strong cup of freshly brewed tea.

COOK'S TIP To toast nuts, spread them in a single layer on a baking sheet. Bake in a preheated 375°F oven until golden brown, eight to ten minutes, shaking the pan occasionally.

Per serving:
304 Calories • 7 g Total Fat • 4 g Saturated Fat • 1 mg Cholesterol • 24 mg Sodium • 54 g Total Carbohydrate
5 g Dietary Fiber • 7 g Protein • 79 mg Calcium

6 POINTS per serving

Summer Borscht

The ever-popular Eastern European beet soup, borscht, comes in countless varieties. It can be made with or without meat, served hot or cold, and may include cabbage or other vegetables. It is often served with a dollop of sour cream on top, but in this light uncooked version, sour cream is mixed into the soup for a creamier texture. Chill before serving if desired.

*Makes 4 servings
(yield 4 cups)*

2 (15-ounce) cans small whole beets, rinsed and drained

1 (13³/4-ounce) can vegetable broth

¹/2 cup light sour cream

3 tablespoons balsamic or red wine vinegar

¹/2 cup chopped fresh dill

¹/4 teaspoon salt

¹/3 cup peeled, seeded, and diced cucumber

4 dill sprigs

Puree the beets, broth, sour cream, vinegar, dill, and salt in a food processor or blender. Pour into bowls. Top each serving with cucumber and a dill sprig.

What's for Lunch

Whole rye crisp breads spread with a little goat cheese and topped with a thin slice of smoked salmon are a tasty accompaniment.

Per serving:
105 Calories • 4 g Total Fat • 2 g Saturated Fat • 12 mg Cholesterol • 961 mg Sodium • 15 g Total Carbohydrate
3 g Dietary Fiber • 3 g Protein • 60 mg Calcium

2 POINTS per serving

Chilled Tomato-Cucumber Soup

Makes 4 servings
(yield 5 cups)

3 tomatoes, seeded and coarsely chopped

1 cucumber, peeled, seeded, and diced

$1/4$ cup chopped red onion

$1/4$ cup chopped fresh cilantro

2 tablespoons chopped drained pimiento

1 cup mixed vegetable juice

$1/4$ cup reduced-sodium chicken broth

2 tablespoons balsamic vinegar

1 tablespoon extra-virgin olive oil

$1/2$ teaspoon hot pepper sauce

$1/2$ teaspoon salt

Make this refreshing gazpacho-like soup in summer, when tomatoes are at their peak. Substitute fresh basil instead of cilantro if you prefer, and up the ration of hot pepper sauce if you like things really hot and spicy.

Puree the tomatoes in a food processor or blender. Add the cucumber, onion, cilantro, and pimiento; pulse until pureed. Add the vegetable juice, broth, vinegar, oil, pepper sauce, and salt; process to blend. Cover and chill at least an hour before serving.

What's for Lunch

Team this cold soup with mini corn muffins and a slice or two of reduced-fat Monterey Jack cheese. Garnish the soup with colorful chopped red, green, and yellow bell peppers.

1 POINT per serving

Per serving:
76 Calories • 4 g Total Fat • 1 g Saturated Fat • 0 mg Cholesterol • 505 mg Sodium • 10 g Total Carbohydrate
2 g Dietary Fiber • 2 g Protein • 22 mg Calcium

Chilled Tomato-Cucumber Soup

Cool Fruit Soup

Refreshing and tangy, this soup works with almost any combination of fruit. The sugar adds a subtle sweetness, but if you prefer, you can omit it. If you need to save time, look for precut melon at your local market or salad bar. We suggest using gala apples or another sweet eating variety.

Makes 2 servings
(yield 2 cups)

2¹/₂ cups seeded and chopped honeydew melon (about ¹/₂ melon)

1 apple, peeled, cored, and chopped

¹/₄ cup loosely packed fresh mint leaves

2 tablespoons fresh lime juice

2 tablespoons sugar

1 teaspoon grated lime zest

¹/₄ cup halved seedless red grapes

Puree the melon, apple, mint, lime juice, sugar, and lime zest in a blender or food processor. Pour into serving bowls and garnish with the grapes.

What's for Lunch

Keep this menu no-cook by serving the soup with crisp flatbread and reduced-fat cheddar cheese.

COOK'S TIP If you have time, make the soup ahead and store it overnight in the refrigerator; it actually tastes better the next day, after the flavors have had time to meld.

3 POINTS per serving

Per serving:
182 Calories • 1 g Total Fat • 0 g Saturated Fat • 0 mg Cholesterol • 25 mg Sodium • 47 g Total Carbohydrate
3 g Dietary Fiber • 2 g Protein • 32 mg Calcium

Thai Fruit Salad

The refreshing flavors of basil and mint, so common in Thai cooking, bring out the best of this fruit medley. The salad could serve equally well as a light summer supper, or as part of a Thai-inspired dinner menu.

**Makes 4 servings
(yield 8 cups)**

2 cups cubed mango

2 cups cubed cantaloupe

2 cups cubed honeydew melon

2 (8-ounce) cans pineapple chunks in juice, drained

1/4 cup thinly sliced fresh basil

2 tablespoons chopped fresh mint

2 tablespoons fresh lime juice

2 teaspoons sugar

2 teaspoons grated lime zest

Combine the mango, cantaloupe, honeydew, pineapple, basil, mint, lime juice, sugar, and lime zest in a large bowl.

What's for Lunch

Serve over shredded iceberg lettuce and top with low–fat vanilla yogurt.

COOK'S TIP Many supermarkets now carry cubed mango, as well as papaya (that could easily be substituted for the mango), in jars in the produce section. To save time, turn to the salad bar in your market for cubed melon.

3 POINTS per serving

Per serving:
163 Calories • 1 g Total Fat • 0 g Saturated Fat • 0 mg Cholesterol • 20 mg Sodium • 42 g Total Carbohydrate
4 g Dietary Fiber • 2 g Protein • 40 mg Calcium

Crunchy Sugar Snap Pea Salad

This colorful salad is brimming with abundant summer vegetables—bright green sugar snap peas, red tomatoes and onion, and orange baby carrots. It makes a great addition to a picnic lunch. Remember that sweet sugar snap peas are completely edible, pod and all.

Makes 6 servings

$1/4$ cup balsamic vinegar

1 tablespoon chopped fresh thyme

1 tablespoon extra-virgin olive oil

1 teaspoon Dijon mustard

$3/4$ teaspoon salt

2 cups sugar snap peas, trimmed

1 cup halved baby carrots

2 tomatoes, seeded and chopped

1 celery stalk, chopped

$1/2$ cup chopped red onion

6 ounces reduced-fat, sharp cheddar cheese, cut into chunks

3 cups mesclun

Whisk together the vinegar, thyme, oil, mustard, and salt in a large bowl. Stir in the peas, carrots, tomatoes, celery, onion, and cheese. Arrange the mesclun on a platter and top with the vegetable mixture.

What's for Lunch

Serve this salad with garlic croutons sprinkled on top.

COOK'S TIP If you like, substitute two (six-ounce) cans tuna, packed in spring water, drained and flaked, for the cheese.

---

3 POINTS per serving

Per serving:
138 Calories • 7 g Total Fat • 3 g Saturated Fat • 15 mg Cholesterol • 492 mg Sodium • 11 g Total Carbohydrate
2 g Dietary Fiber • 10 g Protein • 302 mg Calcium

Couscous-Stuffed Tomatoes

A staple of the North African diet, filling and flavorful couscous has gained popularity in recent years. Most packaged couscous sold in supermarkets is quick-cooking, whether prominently labeled as such or not; check directions and make sure that the couscous will cook in about five minutes.

Makes 6 servings
(yield 6 cups)

1 1/2 cups reduced-sodium chicken broth

1 cup quick-cooking couscous

3 tablespoons orange juice

2 tablespoons cider vinegar

1 tablespoon honey

1 tablespoon olive oil

2 teaspoons Dijon mustard

1/4 teaspoon salt

1 small cucumber, peeled, seeded, and diced

1/2 cup currants or raisins

1/2 cup chopped pitted dates

2 scallions, chopped

3 tablespoons pine nuts

1/2 cup chopped fresh mint

6 large tomatoes

1 Bring the broth to a boil in a saucepan. Stir in the couscous, cover, and remove from the heat. Let stand 5 minutes.

2 Meanwhile, whisk together the orange juice, vinegar, honey, oil, mustard, and salt in a large bowl. Fluff the couscous with a fork and add to the bowl. Stir in the cucumber, raisins, dates, scallions, pine nuts, and mint.

3 Cut each tomato horizontally in half. Scoop out the seeds and pulp, leaving a 1/2-inch border. Spoon the couscous mixture into the tomato halves.

What's for Lunch

Serve the tomatoes with thinly sliced baked ham and reduced-fat Swiss cheese wrapped together to create mini rolls.

COOK'S TIP Make sure to fluff the couscous with a fork immediately after all of the water has been absorbed to prevent clumping. If clumps form, stir in a little of the juice mixture and then fluff.

Per serving:
288 Calories • 5 g Total Fat • 1 g Saturated Fat • 0 mg Cholesterol • 264 mg Sodium • 56 g Total Carbohydrate
6 g Dietary Fiber • 8 g Protein • 58 mg Calcium

5 POINTS per serving

LUNCH

Antipasto Pizza

Two great Italian traditions, and one delicious recipe that has almost infinite flavor variations. For example, try romaine lettuce in place of the iceberg or sprinkle chopped roasted red peppers or sun-dried tomatoes—the packed-in-water variety—on top.

Makes 6 servings

1 (10-ounce) prebaked pizza crust

2 cups shredded iceberg lettuce

1 tomato, seeded and chopped

1/2 red onion, thinly sliced

1 carrot, shredded

3/4 cup peeled, seeded, and chopped cucumber

5 pitted black olives, sliced

2 tablespoons balsamic vinegar

1 1/2 tablespoons extra-virgin olive oil

1/2 teaspoon dried oregano

2 tablespoons grated Parmesan cheese

1 Place the pizza crust directly on an oven rack and turn the oven on to 450°F. Cook 10 minutes and remove from the oven.

2 Meanwhile, combine the lettuce, tomato, onion, carrot, cucumber, olives, vinegar, oil, and oregano in a bowl. Top the pizza crust with the mixture, leaving a 1/2-inch border, and sprinkle with the Parmesan cheese.

What's for Lunch

For a protein boost, serve the pizza with a few strips of leftover cooked lean chicken, turkey, beef, or ham.

4 POINTS per serving

Per serving:
164 Calories • 7 g Total Fat • 1 g Saturated Fat • 4 mg Cholesterol • 283 mg Sodium • 21 g Total Carbohydrate
1 g Dietary Fiber • 6 g Protein • 97 mg Calcium

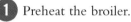

Open-Face Veggie Melts

Bubbly and gooey melts are the ultimate comfort food. Laden with vegetables, our version is healthy, as well as delicious. If you like, substitute reduced-fat extra sharp cheddar for the provolone.

Makes 4 servings

1 teaspoon olive oil

1 onion, thinly sliced

1 garlic clove, minced

2 small zucchini, thinly sliced (about 2 cups)

1 roasted sweet red pepper, drained and thinly sliced

1 teaspoon dried basil

1/2 teaspoon salt

1/4 teaspoon coarsely ground black pepper

4 slices rye bread

2 small tomatoes, each cut into 4 slices

1/4 pound provolone cheese, shredded (about 1 cup)

 Preheat the broiler.

2 Heat the oil in a large nonstick skillet over medium-high heat. Add the onion, garlic, and zucchini. Cover and cook, stirring occasionally, until softened, 3–4 minutes. Add the roasted pepper, basil, salt, and pepper; cook 1 minute longer.

3 Place the bread on a baking sheet. Put 2 tomato slices on each slice of bread; top with equal amounts of the vegetable mixture. Sprinkle with cheese and broil until the cheese melts, about 1 minute.

What's for Lunch

Serve with steaming mugs of reduced-fat cream of celery soup, sprinkled with chopped fresh parsley.

 COOK'S TIP Roasted sweet red peppers in jars are a quick, convenient, and sometimes cheap substitute for fresh red bell peppers. Look for them in your supermarket's Italian section.

Per serving:
225 Calories • 10 g Total Fat • 5 g Saturated Fat • 19 mg Cholesterol • 784 mg Sodium • 24 g Total Carbohydrate
4 g Dietary Fiber • 11 g Protein • 262 mg Calcium

5 POINTS per serving

Berries 'n' Cream Blintzes

Blintzes, the ultimate comfort food, are filled here with a luscious medley of berries in a citrus sauce. Consider spooning this yummy sauce over pancakes, angel food cake, or shortcake. Instead of the typical, high-fat sour cream topping, this berry delight is finished with a light vanilla cream.

Makes 4 servings

1/2 cup orange juice

1 tablespoon fresh lemon juice

2 tablespoons sugar

4 cups mixed berries (blueberries, raspberries, and strawberries)

1/2 cup light sour cream

1/4 teaspoon vanilla extract

4 ready-to-use crêpes

Confectioners' sugar

 Combine the orange juice, lemon juice, and 1 tablespoon of the sugar in a large saucepan. Bring to a boil and cook until the mixture is thick and syrupy, about 5 minutes. Remove from the heat and gently stir in the berries.

 Combine the sour cream, vanilla, and the remaining 1 tablespoon sugar in a small bowl.

3 Spoon 2 tablespoons of the sour cream mixture in the center of each crêpe. Top with equal amounts of the berry mixture. Fold the crêpes up to enclose the filling and dust with confectioners' sugar.

What's for Lunch

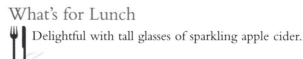 Delightful with tall glasses of sparkling apple cider.

 COOK'S TIP Look for ready-to-use crêpes in your supermarket's produce section. If you use round crêpes, fold the bottom up over the filling, then fold in the sides and roll up the crêpe. If you use square crêpes, fold a corner over the filling to the opposite corner, then fold in half again to form a triangle.

Per serving:
290 Calories • 12 g Total Fat • 4 g Saturated Fat • 114 mg Cholesterol • 200 mg Sodium • 41 g Total Carbohydrate 5 g Dietary Fiber • 8 g Protein • 114 mg Calcium

6 POINTS per serving

Undevilish Eggs

The problem with most deviled eggs is that they contain too much fat and cholesterol-filled egg yolk. This speedy recipe uses just enough of the devilish yolk to flavor the filling, while making the most of the heavenly egg whites. The plastic bag you mix the filling in also does double duty, becoming a pastry bag with which to fill the eggs.

Makes 4 servings

8 hard-cooked large eggs, peeled

2 tablespoons plain nonfat yogurt

1 tablespoon sweet pickle relish

1 teaspoon Dijon mustard

1/2 teaspoon fresh lemon juice

1/4 teaspoon salt

Parsley leaves (optional)

1 Cut the eggs in half lengthwise. Put 2 of the yolks in a large zip-close plastic bag and discard the remaining yolks. Set aside 8 egg white halves and finely chop the remaining 8. Transfer the chopped whites to the plastic bag; add the yogurt, pickle relish, mustard, lemon juice, and salt. Squeeze the bag with your hands until the mixture is well combined.

2 Force the egg mixture into one corner of the plastic bag and snip the corner with scissors or a sharp knife. Fill the reserved egg white halves with the mixture by forcing it out of the plastic bag through the hole. Garnish with parsley leaves if desired.

What's for Lunch

Pair the eggs with spinach salad for a stylishly simple and refreshing lunch.

 COOK'S TIP These eggs are great, not only for a quick lunch, but also as an hors d'oeuvre. If you like your deviled eggs a tad spicy, add a bit of hot Hungarian paprika.

2 POINTS per serving

Per serving:
75 Calories • 3 g Total Fat • 1 g Saturated Fat • 106 mg Cholesterol • 302 mg Sodium • 3 g Total Carbohydrate
0 g Dietary Fiber • 9 g Protein • 33 mg Calcium

LUNCH

Mediterranean Omelet

The timeless combination of tomato and basil, along with intensely flavored Greek kalamata olives, lend an Aegean accent to this omelet. Be sure to buy fat-free egg substitute; some brands contain quite a bit of hidden fat.

Makes 2 servings

1/2 cup chopped tomato

2 tablespoons chopped onion

3 kalamata olives, pitted and chopped

2 tablespoons chopped fresh basil

1 teaspoon balsamic vinegar

1/4 teaspoon salt

1/8 teaspoon coarsely ground black pepper

1 cup fat-free egg substitute

1 tablespoon grated Parmesan cheese

 Combine the tomato, onion, olives, basil, vinegar, salt, and pepper in a bowl.

2 Lightly spray a medium nonstick skillet with nonstick spray; heat over medium heat until a drop of water sizzles. Pour in the egg substitute and swirl to cover the pan. Cook, stirring gently, until the underside begins to set, about 3 minutes. Sprinkle with the cheese and cook 1 minute longer. Spoon the tomato mixture evenly over one side of the omelet; fold the other half over the filling and heat to serving temperature, about 1 minute.

What's for Lunch

For a full and satisfying lunch, serve the omelet with toasted bagels and crisp-cooked turkey bacon.

 For better flavor, buy Parmesan cheese in chunks and grate it as needed. Imported Parmigiano-Reggiano cheese is our favorite.

2 POINTS per serving

Per serving:
97 Calories • 2 g Total Fat • 1 g Saturated Fat • 2 mg Cholesterol • 591 mg Sodium • 6 g Total Carbohydrate
1 g Dietary Fiber • 14 g Protein • 88 mg Calcium

North African Couscous with Chickpeas

Aromatic cumin, coriander, and cinnamon typically blend together in Moroccan cooking. This dish makes a wonderful vegetarian entrée or a robust side dish that will perk up a meal of broiled chicken or fish.

Makes 4 servings (yield 4 cups)

1 1/4 cups water

1 tablespoon olive oil

1 teaspoon ground cumin

1/2 teaspoon ground coriander

1/4 teaspoon ground cinnamon

3/4 teaspoon salt

1/4 teaspoon coarsely ground black pepper

1 cup quick-cooking couscous

1 (15-ounce) can chickpeas, rinsed and drained

2 teaspoons grated lemon zest

Combine the water, oil, cumin, coriander, cinnamon, salt, and pepper in a saucepan. Bring to a boil, remove from the heat, and stir in the couscous. Cover and let stand 5 minutes. Stir in the chickpeas and lemon zest; let stand 2 minutes longer. Fluff with a fork before serving.

What's for Lunch

Stir a little chopped fresh mint or cucumber into plain nonfat yogurt; serve with the couscous.

 COOK'S TIP Leftovers? Cover and refrigerate them; serve them chilled within the next three days.

6 POINTS per serving

Per serving (1 cup):
299 Calories • 5 g Total Fat • 1 g Saturated Fat • 0 mg Cholesterol • 635 mg Sodium • 51 g Total Carbohydrate
7 g Dietary Fiber • 11 g Protein • 51 mg Calcium

Totally Vegetarian Tostadas

Tempeh is a nutty and smoky tasting soybean cake that is very high in protein. It makes an excellent substitute for meat, since you can cook it in the same way you would ground beef. Found in the produce section of the supermarket and in health food stores, it can vary in texture; look for firm tempeh that will crumble easily.

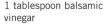

Makes 4 servings

4 (6-inch) corn tortillas

1 teaspoon canola oil

1 (8-ounce) package soy tempeh, crumbled

1 tablespoon taco seasoning mix

1/4 cup water

2 tomatoes, seeded and chopped

1 tablespoon balsamic vinegar

1 (16-ounce) jar fat-free black bean dip

2 cups mixed salad greens or mesclun

1/4 cup light sour cream

2 tablespoons chopped fresh cilantro

1 Preheat the oven to 450°F. Arrange the tortillas in a single layer on a baking sheet and bake until crisp and light brown around the edges, 5–7 minutes.

2 Meanwhile, heat the oil in a nonstick skillet over medium-high heat. Add the tempeh, seasoning mix, and water. Sauté until the liquid evaporates, about 2 minutes. Remove from the heat and stir in the tomatoes and vinegar.

3 Spread each tortilla with bean dip. Divide the tempeh mixture and the greens among the tortillas. Top each with 1 tablespoon sour cream and 1 1/2 teaspoons cilantro.

What's for Lunch

 Serve with a crunchy corn and red pepper salad.

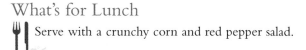 **COOK'S TIP** Tempeh is commonly sold in patties or loaves. It can be cut into chunks, marinated and grilled, than added to soups, vegetable casseroles, and chilis.

7 POINTS per serving

Per serving:
341 Calories • 8 g Total Fat • 2 g Saturated Fat • 6 mg Cholesterol • 643 mg Sodium • 45 g Total Carbohydrate
9 g Dietary Fiber • 22 g Protein • 167 mg Calcium

L
U
N
C
H

Tomatoes Stuffed with Fennel-Flavored Salmon Salad

This easy-to-prepare dish is simple enough to make for a family meal, but elegant enough to serve company. Reserve the top third of each tomato to place on top of the stuffing.

Makes 4 servings (yield 3 cups salad)

4 tomatoes

1 (14³/4-ounce) can red sockeye salmon, drained

¹/2 cup finely chopped fennel bulb

¹/2 cup finely chopped onion

2 small carrots, chopped

¹/4 cup fresh lemon juice

¹/4 cup reduced-fat mayonnaise

2 teaspoons dried tarragon

¹/2 teaspoon coarsely ground black pepper

1 Slice off the top third of each tomato, set aside. Scoop out and discard the seeds and inner flesh with a small spoon.

2 Combine the salmon, fennel, onion, carrots, lemon juice, mayonnaise, tarragon, and pepper in a bowl. Fill each tomato with ³/4 cup of the salad, mounding if necessary. Top each with tomato slices.

What's for Lunch

 Make it a French experience by serving this stuffed "love apple" on a bed of Belgian endive with a crusty baguette.

COOK'S TIP When you have time over the weekend, chop onions and refrigerate in tightly sealed plastic bags for quick use during the week.

4 POINTS per serving

Per serving:
202 Calories • 10 g Total Fat • 2 g Saturated Fat • 25 mg Cholesterol • 479 mg Sodium • 13 g Total Carbohydrate 3 g Dietary Fiber • 15 g Protein • 211 mg Calcium

L U N C H

Salmon 'n' Cress Sandwiches

These delicate and delightful sandwiches have a surprisingly robust flavor, thanks to the peppery watercress and the horseradish. Don't bother picking out the tiny bones sprinkled through canned salmon; they are soft, edible, and a good source of calcium, although you may want to remove the more prominent pin bone.

**Makes 4 servings
(yield 2 cups)**

1 (14³/4-ounce) can red sockeye salmon, drained

3 tablespoons reduced-calorie mayonnaise

2 tablespoons capers, drained and chopped

2 tablespoons chopped fresh dill, or 2 teaspoons dried

1 tablespoon prepared horseradish

2 teaspoons grated lemon zest

1 teaspoon coarse-grained Dijon mustard

4 pumpernickel or whole-wheat rolls, split

¹/2 bunch watercress, stemmed and rinsed (about 2 cups)

1 tomato, cut into 8 slices

1 Combine the salmon, mayonnaise, capers, dill, horseradish, lemon zest, and mustard in a bowl.

2 Layer the bottom half of each roll with ¹/2 cup watercress, 2 tomato slices, and ¹/2 cup salmon salad. Top with tops of the rolls and cut the sandwiches in half.

What's for Lunch

 Serve the sandwiches with a sliced cucumber and dill salad and finish with fresh fruit.

COOK'S TIP For a quick hors d'oeuvre, mound salmon salad on reduced-fat butter crackers or toasted black bread triangles; top each with a caper and dill sprig.

6 POINTS per serving

Per serving:
306 Calories • 12 g Total Fat • 2 g Saturated Fat • 18 mg Cholesterol • 865 mg Sodium • 32 g Total Carbohydrate
4 g Dietary Fiber • 19 g Protein • 259 mg Calcium

Sardine, Cucumber, and Watercress Sandwich

Nutritious sardines are an often-overlooked food, despite the fact that they are assertively flavorful and a rich source of omega-3 fatty acids, potassium, calcium, and phosphorus. Serve them in this tasty, easy sandwich, set off by creamy Neufchâtel cheese and peppery watercress.

Makes 4 servings

2 (3³/4-ounce) cans sardines in spring water, drained

2 tablespoons fresh lemon juice

1 ¹/2 teaspoons olive oil

1 teaspoon dried oregano

¹/2 teaspoon salt

4 ounces Neufchâtel cheese, at room temperature

8 slices pumpernickel bread

¹/2 bunch watercress, stemmed and washed (about 2 cups)

¹/2 small cucumber, peeled and thinly sliced

Mash the sardines in a bowl. Add the lemon juice, oil, oregano, and salt and stir until blended. Spread the cheese on 4 slices of bread. Layer an equal amount of watercress, sardine mixture, and cucumber slices over the cheese and cover the sandwiches with the remaining slices of bread. Cut the sandwiches in half.

What's for Lunch

Serve with your favorite oven-baked chips.

7 POINTS per serving

Per serving:
335 Calories • 14 g Total Fat • 6 g Saturated Fat • 40 mg Cholesterol • 1,039 mg Sodium • 33 g Total Carbohydrate 5 g Dietary Fiber • 21 g Protein • 244 mg Calcium

LUNCH

Shrimp Salad Sandwiches

Shrimp salad makes a savvy change of pace from everyday tuna or chicken salad. This salad owes its distinctive flavor to Thai fish sauce, now readily available in the Asian section of most markets. If you can't find it, substitute slightly less pungent soy sauce.

Makes 4 servings

1/4 cup fresh lime juice

2 tablespoons chopped fresh cilantro

2 tablespoons chopped fresh mint

1 tablespoon Thai fish sauce

2 teaspoons sugar

3/4 pound frozen cooked baby shrimp, thawed

1/2 cup seeded and chopped red bell pepper

1/2 medium cucumber, peeled, seeded, and cut into thin strips

1 large scallion, chopped

4 (6 1/2-inch) pita bread rounds

1 Combine the lime juice, cilantro, mint, fish sauce and sugar in a bowl. Stir in the shrimp, bell pepper, cucumber, and scallion.

2 Cut off the top third of each pita bread and discard. Fill each pocket with 1/4 of the salad mixture.

What's for Lunch

 Broiled pineapple rings nicely complement these sandwiches.

 COOK'S TIP To thaw frozen shrimp quickly, simply put them in a strainer placed under cool running water for three to four minutes.

4 POINTS per serving

Per serving:
234 Calories • 2 g Total Fat • 0 g Saturated Fat • 166 mg Cholesterol • 783 mg Sodium • 31 g Total Carbohydrate • 2 g Dietary Fiber • 23 g Protein • 92 mg Calcium

Tomato-Studded Tuna Salad Sandwiches

These tuna sandwiches are chock-full of garden vegetables. If you like, substitute sliced cooked chicken breast or canned salmon for the tuna.

Makes 4 servings
(yield 1¹/2 cups salad)

1 (6-ounce) can solid white tuna in spring water, drained

¹/2 cup seeded and chopped tomatoes

¹/4 cup chopped celery

1 small carrot, chopped

3 tablespoons reduced-fat mayonnaise

2 tablespoons finely chopped onion

1 tablespoon capers, drained

1 tablespoon red wine vinegar

2 kaiser rolls, spilt horizontally

Mix the tuna, tomatoes, celery, carrots, mayonnaise, onion, capers, and vinegar in a bowl. Spread ³/4-cup of the salad on the bottom of each roll, add the tops, and cut the sandwiches in half.

What's for Lunch

Serve the sandwiches with jarred marinated mushrooms and crunchy coleslaw.

 COOK'S TIP To make the coleslaw a snap, buy prepackaged coleslaw mix in the produce section of your market; drizzle with fat-free Italian vinaigrette.

Per serving:
158 Calories • 3 g Total Fat • 0 g Saturated Fat • 16 mg Cholesterol • 491 mg Sodium • 21 g Total Carbohydrate
1 g Dietary Fiber • 13 g Protein • 37 mg Calcium

3 POINTS per serving

Chicken with Tomatoes and Mozzarella

Makes 4 servings

3/4 pound cooked chicken breast, skinned and sliced

4 ounces part-skim mozzarella cheese, sliced

1 pint grape tomatoes, halved

10 kalamata olives, pitted and coarsely chopped

3 tablespoons chopped fresh oregano, or 1 table- spoon dried

1/2 teaspoon salt

1/2 teaspoon coarsely ground black pepper

1/2 cup coarsely chopped fresh basil

This classic Italian salad combination provides a welcome setting for cold chicken in this summertime no-cook lunch or dinner. Purchase cooked chicken breasts from the supermarket or use leftovers. If you can't find the smaller, sweeter grape tomatoes, use cherry tomatoes. For a slightly more intense flavor, use smoked mozzarella.

Alternately arrange slices of chicken and mozzarella around a large platter. Scatter tomatoes and olives over the platter. Sprinkle with the oregano, salt, pepper, and basil. Cover and refrigerate until ready to use.

What's for Lunch

This Italian platter is perfect with hunks of ciabatta or other crusty bread.

5 POINTS per serving

Per serving:
244 Calories • 9 g Total Fat • 4 g Saturated Fat • 88 mg Cholesterol • 575 mg Sodium • 6 g Total Carbohydrate
1g Dietary Fiber • 34 g Protein • 225 mg Calcium

South-of-the-Border Chicken Salad with Key Lime Dressing

Make this Tex-Mex salad using leftover chicken or roasted chicken from your deli counter. It's topped with a pungent dressing made from the smaller, rounder key limes native to Florida. If you can't find fresh key limes, bottled key lime juice will do.

Makes 6 servings
(yield 7 cups)

3 tablespoons key lime juice

2 tablespoons taco sauce

2 tablespoons olive oil

1 tablespoon canned chopped mild green chiles, drained

3/4 teaspoon salt

1/2 teaspoon ground cumin

3 cups sliced cooked chicken breasts

1 bunch watercress, stemmed and washed

1 cup cherry or grape tomatoes, halved

6 scallions, thinly sliced on the diagonal

1/2 cup chopped fresh cilantro

Whisk together the lime juice, taco sauce, oil, chiles, salt, and cumin in a large bowl until blended. Stir in the chicken, watercress, tomatoes, scallions, and cilantro.

What's for Lunch

Serve with a basket of reduced-fat tortilla chips.

COOK'S TIP Cilantro has an intense, unique flavor that adds delicious—and distinctive—taste to Asian and Latin American cuisine. Look for cilantro with bright green leaves that give off a strong fragrance when you rub them between your fingers.

Per serving (generous 1 cup):
175 Calories • 7 g Total Fat • 1 g Saturated Fat • 60 mg Cholesterol • 391 mg Sodium • 4 g Total Carbohydrate • 1 g Dietary Fiber • 23 g Protein • 61 mg Calcium

4 POINTS per serving

Curried Turkey Salad

In this different take on the classic Waldorf salad, you can easily substitute cubed cooked chicken for the turkey, or make the salad vegetarian by using firm tofu. The salad also can be made into a delicious sandwich.

Makes 4 servings
(yield 4 cups)

1/2 cup light mayonnaise

1/4 cup mango chutney

1 tablespoon curry powder

1 teaspoon Dijon mustard

1/2 teaspoon coarsely ground black pepper

2 cups cubed cooked turkey breast

2 celery stalks, chopped

1 apple, cored and chopped

6 scallions, thinly sliced

1/2 cup chopped walnuts

1/4 cup raisins

Whisk together the mayonnaise, chutney, curry powder, mustard, and pepper in a large bowl. Stir in the turkey, celery, apple, scallions, walnuts, and raisins. Cover and chill before serving.

What's for Lunch

Serve over romaine lettuce leaves with multigrain toast triangles.

 COOK'S TIP Curry powder loses its flavor over time. Make sure you buy a new jar every few years.

9 POINTS per serving

Per serving:
399 Calories • 22 g Total Fat • 3 g Saturated Fat • 59 mg Cholesterol • 356 mg Sodium • 27 g Total Carbohydrate
4 g Dietary Fiber • 26 g Protein • 73 mg Calcium

Turkey, Swiss, and Pear Wraps

Wraps are a stylishly simple alternative to the everyday sandwich. Sweet and spicy honey mustard provides a welcome foil to peppery arugula. Choose a ripe Anjou, Bartlett, or Comice pear for the sweetest, most succulent flavor.

Makes 4 servings

4 (8-inch) reduced-fat flour tortillas

1/4 cup honey mustard

1 cup loosely packed arugula leaves

1/2 pound deli-sliced turkey breast

1/4 pound deli-sliced reduced-fat Swiss cheese

1 pear, cored and thinly sliced

Spread one side of each tortilla with 1 tablespoon of the honey mustard. Divide the arugula, turkey, cheese, and pears among the tortillas. Fold opposite sides of each tortilla up around the filling to form a cone and secure with toothpicks.

What's for Lunch

Serve each wrap with a small bunch of red or green grapes

Per serving:
362 Calories • 9 g Total Fat • 3 g Saturated Fat • 62 mg Cholesterol • 716 mg Sodium • 43 g Total Carbohydrate
11 g Dietary Fiber • 30 g Protein • 349 mg Calcium

7 POINTS per serving

LUNCH

Turkey Reuben Sandwiches

Who says the Reuben sandwich (named for a Manhattan restaurateur), one of our quintessential comfort foods, has to be off limits? To pare the fat grams, we use turkey breast, fat-free dressing, and reduced-fat Swiss cheese.

Makes 2 servings

4 slices rye bread

4 teaspoons prepared mustard

4 tablespoons fat-free Thousand Island dressing

6 tablespoons sauerkraut, well drained

6 ounces deli-sliced turkey breast

2 (1-ounce) slices reduced-fat Swiss cheese

 1 Preheat the oven or toaster oven to 400°F.

2 Spread 1 side of each slice of bread with 1 teaspoon of the mustard and 1 tablespoon of the Thousand Island dressing. Divide the sauerkraut and turkey between 2 of the slices. Top each with 1 slice of the Swiss cheese and 1 of the remaining slices of bread.

3 Place the sandwiches on a baking sheet or toaster oven tray and bake until the cheese melts and the sandwiches are hot, about 6 minutes.

What's for Lunch

This filling treat is set off nicely by a salad of sliced tomatoes.

 COOK'S TIP Rinsing and then squeezing excess liquid from the sauerkraut will help cut the sodium content.

8 *POINTS* per serving

Per serving:
411 Calories • 7 g Total Fat • 3 g Saturated Fat • 86 mg Cholesterol • 1,085 mg Sodium • 42 g Total Carbohydrate • 6 g Dietary Fiber • 40 g Protein • 369 mg Calcium

Turkey Reuben Sandwiches

Turkey Bacon Cheeseburger

A simple, healthy version of this classic American favorite, our recipe pares down the fat by using lean ground chicken breast, reduced-fat cheddar cheese and turkey bacon. Don't forget to toast the rolls!

Makes 4 servings

1 pound ground skinless chicken breast

2 tablespoons ketchup

2 tablespoons plain dried bread crumbs

2 teaspoons Dijon mustard

1/2 cup shredded reduced-fat cheddar cheese

4 hamburger rolls

4 strips crisp-cooked turkey bacon, halved

4 leaf-lettuce leaves (optional)

4 slices tomato (optional)

4 slices white onion (optional)

1 Combine the chicken, ketchup, bread crumbs, and mustard in a bowl. With moistened hands, shape the mixture into four 1/2-inch thick patties. Coat a large nonstick skillet with nonstick spray and heat over medium-high heat. Put the patties in the skillet, cover, and cook until cooked through, about 4 minutes on each side.

2 Sprinkle the burgers with the shredded cheese, cover, and cook until melted, about 1 minute longer. Serve the burgers in the hamburger rolls, topping each with a strip of bacon. Garnish with lettuce leaves, tomato slices, and onion slices if desired.

What's for Lunch

Pair the burgers with another classic American favorite—a cup of soothing tomato soup (make it the reduced-fat variety).

COOK'S TIP The fastest way to cook bacon is in the microwave. Place the strips on a paper towel and microwave on High until crisp-cooked, approximately two-and-a-half to three minutes.

9 *POINTS* per serving

Per serving:
377 Calories • 17 g Total Fat • 2 g Saturated Fat • 11 mg Cholesterol • 741 mg Sodium • 27 g Total Carbohydrate
2 g Dietary Fiber • 29 g Protein • 143 mg Calcium

Roast Beef and Arugula Sandwiches with Horseradish Cream

The city of Buffalo's beloved sandwich is nicknamed "beef on weck," and features thinly sliced roast beef spiked with horseradish served on kimelweck rolls, a type of kaiser roll. We serve our version on hearty pumpernickel. Choose the leanest roast beef your deli stocks (eye-round would be ideal); ask that it be sliced as thinly as possible. If arugula is not available, watercress makes an excellent substitute.

Makes 4 servings

3 tablespoons light sour cream

1 tablespoon prepared horseradish, drained

1 tablespoon Dijon mustard

1/8 teaspoon salt

1/8 teaspoon coarsely ground black pepper

2 cups loosely packed arugula

8 slices pumpernickel bread

1/2 pound very thinly sliced lean deli roast beef

1 large tomato, thinly sliced

1 small red onion, thinly sliced

1 Combine the sour cream, horseradish, mustard, salt, and pepper in a small bowl.

2 Put 1/2 cup arugula on each of 4 slices of the bread; divide the roast beef, tomato, and onion among the sandwiches. Top each with horseradish cream and the remaining bread slices. Cut the sandwiches in half on the diagonal.

What's for Lunch

Delicious served with roasted sweet red peppers.

COOK'S TIP For open-faced appetizer sandwiches, cut the bread into triangles, spread with a little horseradish cream, and layer with the remaining ingredients. To top with a Parmesan garnish, shave curls from a wedge of cheese using a vegetable peeler.

Per serving:

6 *POINTS* per serving 293 Calories • 7 g Total Fat • 2 g Saturated Fat • 44 mg Cholesterol • 574 mg Sodium • 35 g Total Carbohydrate
5 g Dietary Fiber • 23 g Protein • 87 mg Calcium

LUNCH

Roast Beef Gyro

The equivalent to Greek fast food, gyro is traditionally made with slowly roasted lamb. Our lighter version, made with lean deli beef, is ready in an instant. It packs plenty of flavor and is served with tzatziki, *the classic cucumber-yogurt sauce.*

Makes 4 servings

2/3 cup plain nonfat yogurt

1/2 cup grated, peeled and seeded cucumber, squeezed dry

1 garlic clove, minced

2 teaspoons extra-virgin olive oil

4 (6 1/2-inch) pita bread rounds

2 cups shredded lettuce

3/4 pound deli-sliced lean roast beef

1 tomato, seeded and chopped

1/2 cup thinly sliced red onion

1 Combine the yogurt, cucumber, garlic, and oil in a small bowl.

2 Lay the pita rounds flat (do not split open). Divide the lettuce and then the beef among the rounds. Top each with 1/4-cup of the tomato and 2 tablespoons of the onion. Drizzle with the yogurt sauce and fold up to eat.

What's for Lunch

A generous green salad with a sprinkling of crumbled feta cheese makes a meal of this tasty snack.

 COOK'S TIP If the taste of raw onions lingers and bothers you, try chewing on a few parsley sprigs afterward to freshen your breath.

9 POINTS per serving

Per serving:
429 Calories • 15 g Total Fat • 5 g Saturated Fat • 70 mg Cholesterol • 421 mg Sodium • 41 g Total Carbohydrate
2 g Dietary Fiber • 32 g Protein • 154 mg Calcium

Asian Pear Salad with Jicama and Honey Ham

Makes 2 servings

3 tablespoons cider vinegar

2 tablespoons orange juice

1 tablespoon honey

1 tablespoon olive oil

1 teaspoon Dijon mustard

$1/8$ teaspoon salt

2 Asian pears, peeled, cored, and sliced

1 small jicama, peeled and cut into 2-inch strips

$1/2$ pound piece fat-free honey ham, cut into $1/2$-inch cubes

4 cups mesclun

Juicy Asian pears and crunchy jicama both lend a sweetness to this unique salad which contrasts nicely with the salty ham. It's an abundant salad that can feed a crowd or anchor a buffet. Look for fat-free ham at your supermarket's deli counter and ask for a whole half-pound piece, rather than slices.

Whisk together the vinegar, orange juice, honey, oil, mustard, and salt in a large bowl. Add the pears, jicama, ham, and mesclun; toss to coat.

What's for Lunch

 Mini corn muffins go well with this flavorful dish.

COOK'S TIP The most common Asian pears (sometimes called Chinese pears) found in supermarkets are large, round, and green to yellow. Since their season is late summer through early fall, you may need to substitute another type of firm pear.

4 POINTS per serving

Per serving:
340 Calories • 8 g Total Fat • 0 g Saturated Fat • 36 mg Cholesterol • 1580 mg Sodium • 52 g Total Carbohydrate 16 g Dietary Fiber • 20 g Protein • 72 mg Calcium

Tuscan Bean Salad with Fennel and Radicchio

*Makes 4 servings
(yield 4 cups salad)*

1 (15¹/₂-ounce) can red kidney beans, rinsed and drained

1 (15¹/₂-ounce) can white kidney beans, rinsed and drained

¹/₂ cup chopped fennel bulb

¹/₄ cup chopped white or red onion

¹/₄ cup chopped celery

1 small carrot, chopped

3 tablespoons fresh lemon juice

1 teaspoon grated lemon zest

2 tablespoons extra-virgin olive oil

4 teaspoons chopped fresh sage

¹/₄ teaspoon coarsely ground black pepper

1 head radicchio, shredded (about 4 cups)

Red and white kidney beans (the latter are often labeled as cannelinni beans) take center stage in this Italian-style salad. The salad also boasts a generous helping of fennel, or the prized finocchio*, and is served on a bed of radicchio, another Italian favorite.*

Combine the beans, fennel, onion, celery, carrot, lemon juice, lemon zest, oil, sage, and pepper in a large bowl. Divide the radicchio among 4 plates and top each with 1 cup of the salad.

What's for Dinner

This fresh tasting and satisfying salad is perfect with Italian breadsticks.

COOK'S TIP If fresh sage is unavailable, substitute fresh rosemary, basil, or oregano or one teaspoon dried sage leaves, crumbled.

5 *POINTS* per serving

Per serving:
260 Calories • 8 g Total Fat • 1 g Saturated Fat • 0 mg Cholesterol • 570 mg Sodium • 38 g Total Carbohydrate
15 g Dietary Fiber • 12 g Protein • 87 mg Calcium

Spicy Hummus with Curried Pita Chips

*Makes 4 servings
(yield 2²/₃ cups)*

4 (6¹/2-inch) pita bread rounds, split

2 egg whites, lightly beaten

2 teaspoons curry powder

¹/2 teaspoon salt

2 (15-ounce) cans chickpeas, rinsed and drained

2 tablespoons tahini paste

2 tablespoons fresh lemon juice

2 teaspoons grated lemon zest

2 garlic cloves

1 teaspoon ground cumin

³/4 cup water

2 tablespoons extra-virgin olive oil

¹/2 teaspoon hot pepper sauce

Thick rich hummus, a Middle Eastern delicacy, stands up well to the spicy curried pita chips. This combination usually is served as an appetizer, but the creamy spread is hearty, and satisfying enough to work as a light dinner. If you don't have a toaster oven, place the pita halves on a baking sheet and toast in a preheated 425°F oven for seven to eight minutes.

1 Brush each pita half with beaten egg white; sprinkle with the curry powder and salt. Toast until crisp, about 4 minutes in a toaster oven. Cut each pita half into 8 triangles.

2 Combine the chickpeas, tahini, lemon juice, lemon zest, garlic, and cumin in a food processor. Puree to form a fairly thick paste, about 2 minutes. While running, pour in the water, olive oil, and pepper sauce. Process until smooth, about 1 minute longer. Serve with the curried pita chips.

What's for Dinner

Serve with a heaping platter of crudités (assorted raw vegetables).

COOK'S TIP Most supermarkets now stock tahini, a paste made from ground sesame seeds that has a peanut butter-like consistency. If yours doesn't carry tahini, look in a health-food store.

10 POINTS per serving

Per serving (generous ¹/2 cup):
512 Calories • 12 g Total Fat • 1 g Saturated Fat • 0 mg Cholesterol • 1,030 mg Sodium • 84 g Total Carbohydrate
12 g Dietary Fiber • 19 g Protein • 146 mg Calcium

Black Bean, Corn, and Avocado Salad

*Makes 4 servings
(yield 6 cups)*

1 (30-ounce) can black beans, rinsed and drained

2 cups corn kernels

1 pint cherry tomatoes, halved

1 avocado, chopped

1 jalapeño pepper, seeded and minced (wear gloves to prevent irritation)

1/4 cup fresh lime juice

2 teaspoons grated lime zest

1/4 cup chopped fresh cilantro

1/2 teaspoon salt

This salad makes a delicious centerpiece at an informal buffet. If you're in a time crunch, pair it with packaged baked tortilla chips. Otherwise, try making your own: Cut reduced-fat flour tortillas into strips or triangles and arrange on a sheet of foil. Bake on the middle rack of a preheated 375°F oven until toasted, about five minutes.

Combine the beans, corn, tomatoes, avocado, jalapeño, lime juice, lime zest, cilantro, and salt in a bowl. Serve at once.

What's for Dinner

Serve the salad on a large leaf of curly green lettuce with baked tortilla chips and a favorite Mexican brew.

COOK'S TIP Fresh corn kernels add crunch to the salad; a large ear will yield about one cup of kernels. For convenience or if fresh corn is not available, substitute thawed frozen kernels.

6 POINTS per serving

Per serving (1 1/2 cups):
283 Calories • 9 g Total Fat • 1 g Saturated Fat • 0 mg Cholesterol • 753 mg Sodium • 52 g Total Carbohydrate
16 g Dietary Fiber • 13 g Protein • 84 mg Calcium

Lemony Lentil and Goat Cheese Salad

Makes 4 servings
(yield 2¹/₄ cups salad)

2 tablespoons fresh lemon juice

1 teaspoon grated lemon zest

1 teaspoon extra-virgin olive oil

1 small garlic clove, minced

¹/₄ teaspoon salt

1 (15-ounce) can lentils, rinsed and drained

1 tomato, seeded and chopped

¹/₄ cup chopped red onion

3 tablespoons chopped fresh parsley

2 ounces goat cheese, crumbled

3 cups loosely packed cleaned arugula leaves

Red onion and tomato add a splash of color to this healthy salad, while the lentils lend a good source of protein, fiber, and complex carbohydrates. If you have trouble finding canned lentils in your supermarket, look for them in a health food store or an Italian market. You could also substitute an equal amount of pink or any variety of white beans. If arugula is unavailable, try romaine lettuce.

Combine the lemon juice, lemon zest, oil, garlic, and salt in a bowl. Gently stir in the lentils, tomato, onion, parsley, and goat cheese. Serve over the arugula.

What's for Dinner

Add pizzazz with an assortment of flavored breadsticks, such as onion, pepper, or garlic.

 If possible, use aged goat cheese, which is drier than the regular variety and will crumble more easily.

3 POINTS per serving

Per serving (about ²/₃ cup):
170 Calories • 6 g Total Fat • 3 g Saturated Fat • 11 mg Cholesterol • 374 mg Sodium • 20 g Total Carbohydrate
7 g Dietary Fiber • 11 g Protein • 91 mg Calcium

DINNER

Pepper Jack Cheese and Spinach Quesadillas

Makes 4 servings

1/2 cup chunked avocado

1 tablespoon fresh lime juice

1/4 teaspoon salt

4 (8-inch) reduced-fat flour tortillas

1 (10-ounce) package frozen chopped spinach, thawed and squeezed dry

2 tablespoons sliced pickled jalapeño, drained

2 tablespoons fresh cilantro leaves

1/4 pound (about 1 cup) reduced-fat Monterey Jack cheese, shredded

You can change this versatile Southwestern treat to suit your mood. You can substitute sautéed sliced mushrooms or rinsed and drained canned beans for the spinach, or add shredded cooked chicken breast. Look for a dark-skinned Hass avocado, which is more flavorful than the lighter green Fuerte variety.

1 Put the avocado, lime juice, and salt into a bowl; mash with a fork. Over one half of each tortilla spread about 1/4 of the avocado mixture, 1/4 of the spinach, 1 1/2 teaspoons jalapeño, 1 1/2 teaspoons cilantro, and 1/4-cup cheese. Fold the bare half of each tortilla over the filling.

2 Heat a dry, nonstick skillet over medium heat. Two at a time, heat the quesadillas in the skillet until the cheese melts and the tortillas are slightly browned, about 3 minutes on each side.

What's for Dinner

All these quesadillas need are a fresh green salad sprinkled with a few crushed fat-free tortilla chips. Serve with a chipotle salsa—if you can stand the heat.

COOK'S TIP Sliced pickled jalapeños are sometimes labeled jalapeño nacho slices. Find them in the ethnic food section of your market. Tortillas vary widely in fat content so be sure to choose the reduced-fat variety. To serve the quesadillas as appetizers, cut them into strips.

4 POINTS **per serving**

Per serving:
226 Calories • 9 g Total Fat • 4 g Saturated Fat • 18 mg Cholesterol • 746 mg Sodium • 26 g Total Carbohydrate
11 g Dietary Fiber • 14 g Protein • 346 mg Calcium

Health Nut Sandwich

One bite of this juicy, crunchy vegetarian sandwich will dispel any reservations you may have about "health food." For variety, try the array of sprouts that now grace most produce aisles in place of alfalfa sprouts; radish sprouts, for example, make for a particularly zesty sandwich.

Makes 4 servings

1/4 cup light mayonnaise

8 slices whole-grain bread, toasted

1 firm, ripe avocado, peeled and thinly sliced

8 ounces firm tofu, sliced

1 large tomato, thinly sliced

1/2 teaspoon salt

1/2 teaspoon coarsely ground black pepper

1 1/2 cups alfalfa sprouts

Spread 1 tablespoon of the mayonnaise on each of 4 slices of toast. Divide and layer the avocado, tofu, and tomato on the sandwiches. Sprinkle with salt and pepper and mound with sprouts. Top each with 1 of the remaining toast slices and cut the sandwiches in half on the diagonal.

What's for Dinner

Pair this sandwich with a green salad mixed with pear slices and apples.

COOK'S TIP To pit and peel an avocado, hold the avocado in one hand. Run a sharp knife lengthwise around the avocado, turning only the avocado, not the knife. Twist the two halves apart. Using the edge of a your knife, make a quick downward stroke into the pit, twist, and remove it. Cut each avocado half lengthwise in two, then peel away the skin.

7 POINTS per serving

Per serving:
343 Calories • 17 g Total Fat • 2 g Saturated Fat • 5 mg Cholesterol • 760 mg Sodium • 44 g Total Carbohydrate
9 g Dietary Fiber • 14 g Protein • 404 mg Calcium

Tofu Teriyaki

Low in saturated fat, cholesterol-free, and high in protein, it's no wonder versatile tofu is becoming a popular choice among health-conscious cooks. We serve it here in a succulent teriyaki sauce—a seasoned soy sauce mixture often used with beef or chicken, surrounded by a fresh vegetable assortment. If you like, you can substitute precooked chicken for the tofu.

*Makes 4 servings
(yield 4 cups + 2 cups
rice)*

1¹/₂ cups quick-cooking rice

¹/₄ cup reduced-sodium soy sauce

2 tablespoons rice vinegar

1 tablespoon sugar

2 teaspoons cornstarch

¹/₄ teaspoon crushed red pepper

1 teaspoon Asian (dark) sesame oil

2 garlic cloves, minced

1 pound bag precut vegetables for stir-fry

1 pound firm tofu, cut into ¹/₂-inch cubes

 Prepare the rice according to package directions, omitting the addition of any fat.

 Combine the soy sauce, vinegar, sugar, cornstarch, and crushed red pepper flakes in a small bowl.

 Heat the oil in a large nonstick skillet over medium–high heat. Add the garlic and cook 30 seconds. Add the vegetables and cook, stirring often, until they begin to soften slightly, about 3 minutes. Add the tofu and cook, stirring occasionally, 3 minutes. Stir in the soy sauce mixture and bring to a boil; cook until thickened, about 2 minutes longer. Serve over the rice.

What's for Dinner

 Serve with iced fruit tea or iced chai, a blend of tea, milk, and spices.

COOK'S TIP If your market doesn't carry bags of assorted vegetables precut for stir-fry, create your own mixture from baby carrots, sliced onion, broccoli florets, and bell pepper strips from the salad bar.

5 *POINTS* per serving

Per serving:
258 Calories • 6 g Total Fat • 1 g Saturated Fat • 0 mg Cholesterol • 557 mg Sodium • 35 g Total Carbohydrate
2 g Dietary Fiber • 16 g Protein • 224 mg Calcium

Pierogies with Creamy Mushroom and Sherry Sauce

Makes 4 servings

1 teaspoon olive oil

2 cups sliced mushrooms

1 onion, sliced

$1/4$ teaspoon salt

$1/4$ teaspoon coarsely ground black pepper

2 tablespoons dry sherry wine

1 tablespoon all-purpose flour

$2/3$ cup low-fat (1%) milk

$1/4$ cup reduced-sodium chicken broth

1 (1-pound) package frozen low-fat potato pierogies, thawed

2 tablespoons light sour cream

A Polish specialty, pierogies are half-moon-shaped dumplings traditionally made with a variety of fillings, including potato, cabbage, or cheese. Frozen pierogies come in various flavors, any of which would be suitable in this recipe. Here we serve them in a silky, sherry-spiked sauce. Most of the packages of frozen precooked pierogies in your supermarket are relatively low in fat, but look for those specifically labeled "low-fat."

Heat the oil in a large nonstick skillet over medium-high heat. Add the mushrooms, onion, salt, and pepper. Cook, stirring occasionally, until the mushrooms and onion are tender and lightly browned, about 4 minutes. Stir in the sherry and cook until evaporated. Sprinkle the flour over the mushroom mixture, stirring to combine. Stir in the milk, broth, and pierogies; bring to a boil. Remove from heat and stir in the sour cream.

What's for Dinner

Serve the pierogies with steamed green beans and applesauce on the side.

 COOK'S TIP You can thaw the pierogies quickly in boiling water for three to five minutes, uncovered; drain before proceeding with the recipe.

5 *POINTS* per serving

Per serving:
249 Calories • 5 g Total Fat • 2 g Saturated Fat • 14 mg Cholesterol • 634 mg Sodium • 42 g Total Carbohydrate
3 g Dietary Fiber • 10 g Protein • 108 mg Calcium

Pan-Seared Salmon with Fresh Tomato-Basil Relish

Makes 2 servings

2 tomatoes, seeded and chopped

1/4 cup thinly sliced fresh basil

1 small garlic clove, minced

1 tablespoon balsamic vinegar

3/4 teaspoon salt

1/4 teaspoon coarsely ground black pepper

2 (6-ounce) salmon fillets, skin on

1/4 teaspoon ground cumin

1/2 teaspoon olive oil

Perfect for a special soiree for two, this elegant dinner can easily be prepared at the end of a busy day. Pan-searing the salmon seals in the juices, leaving the fish succulent and moist. This dish is best in the summer, when fresh tomatoes are at their peak; otherwise, use Roma tomatoes or quartered cherry tomatoes.

1 Combine the tomatoes, basil, garlic, vinegar, 1/2 teaspoon of the salt, and 1/8 teaspoon of the pepper in a small bowl.

2 Sprinkle the salmon with the cumin and the remaining 1/4 teaspoon salt and 1/8 teaspoon pepper. Heat the oil in a nonstick skillet over medium-high heat. Add the salmon, skin-side up, and cook 4 minutes. Turn the salmon and cook 1 minute longer. Cover the pan, reduce heat to medium, and cook until the salmon is just opaque in the center and flakes easily, 2–3 minutes.

3 Transfer the salmon to serving plates and add the tomato mixture to the skillet. Increase the heat to high and cook until the mixture is warmed through, 1–2 minutes. Spoon the relish over the salmon. Avoid eating the salmon skin.

What's for Dinner

 Orzo pasta, lightly drizzled with extra-virgin olive oil and cracked black pepper, makes a fitting accompaniment for this elegant dish.

 COOK'S TIP Store tomatoes, summer or winter varieties, stem-side up at room temperature. Never refrigerate them, as cold destroys their texture and flavor.

8 POINTS per serving

Per serving:
350 Calories • 19 g Total Fat • 4 g Saturated Fat • 89 mg Cholesterol • 976 mg Sodium • 10 g Total Carbohydrate • 2 g Dietary Fiber • 33 g Protein • 44 mg Calcium

Pan-Seared Salmon with Fresh Tomato-Basil Relish

Salmon with Brown Sugar Glaze

Salmon is a good source of high-quality protein and heart-healthy omega-3 fatty acids, making it a healthy and delicious dinner choice. The glaze for this salmon dish is made in a flash with a few kitchen staples. Try it on chicken and pork, too.

Makes 4 servings

1/4 cup packed light brown sugar

2 tablespoons Dijon mustard

2 tablespoons chopped fresh dill, or 2 teaspoons dried

4 (6-ounce) salmon fillets, skinned

1/2 teaspoon salt

1/2 teaspoon coarsely ground black pepper

1 Spray the rack of a broiler pan with nonstick spray; preheat the broiler.

2 Whisk together the brown sugar, mustard, and dill in a small bowl. Sprinkle both sides of the salmon with salt and pepper. Place the salmon on the broiler rack and spoon the brown sugar glaze on top. Position 7 inches from the heat and broil until lightly browned and just opaque in the center, about 6 minutes.

What's for Dinner

Steamed broccoli and rice go well with this dish.

 COOK'S TIP Don't turn the salmon as it broils; you want the glazed side to remain facing the heat to produce an appealing golden brown color.

Per serving:
339 Calories • 17 g Total Fat • 3 g Saturated Fat • 85 mg Cholesterol • 421 mg Sodium • 14 g Total Carbohydrate
0 g Dietary Fiber • 30 g Protein • 44 mg Calcium

8 POINTS per serving

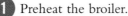

Broiled Scallops Persillade

The French term persillade *isn't a complicated culinary technique, but rather a simple parsley and garlic combination, sometimes mixed with bread crumbs.*

Makes 4 servings

1/4 cup plain dried
bread crumbs

1 tablespoon chopped
fresh parsley

1 garlic clove, minced

1 tablespoon butter, melted

1 teaspoon fresh
lemon juice

Pinch of cayenne

1 1/4 pounds sea scallops

1 Preheat the broiler.

2 Combine the bread crumbs, parsley, garlic, butter, lemon juice, and cayenne in a large bowl. Add the scallops and toss to coat. Place the scallops on the rack of a broiler pan and lightly spray them with non-stick spray. Broil 4 inches from the heat until golden brown on the outside and opaque in the middle, about 4 minutes (do not turn).

What's for Dinner

The scallops pair well with boiled small red potatoes and a steamed green vegetable, such as spinach or broccoli.

 COOK'S TIP The peak season for fresh sea scallops is mid-fall to mid-spring. If you can't find fresh, substitute frozen, which are available year-round.

4 POINTS per serving

Per serving:
182 Calories • 5 g Total Fat • 2 g Saturated Fat • 55 mg Cholesterol • 318 mg Sodium • 9 mg Total Carbohydrate
0 g Dietary Fiber • 25 g Protein • 53 mg Calcium

DINNER

Corn, Tomato, and Shrimp Sauté

This dish makes use of summer's best—fresh corn, tomatoes, and basil. To save time, consider purchasing precleaned (but not cooked) shrimp at your fish market.

Makes 4 servings (yield 4 cups)

2¹/₂ tablespoons olive oil

1 pound peeled and deveined medium shrimp

2 garlic cloves, minced

¹/₂ cup chopped onion

1¹/₂ cups fresh corn kernels (from 2 ears of corn)

2 cups cherry tomatoes

¹/₂ cup chopped fresh basil

¹/₄ teaspoon salt

¹/₄ teaspoon coarsely ground black pepper

1 Heat 2 tablespoons of the oil in a medium nonstick skillet over medium-high heat. Add the shrimp and cook until lightly golden, about 2 minutes on each side. Transfer the shrimp to a plate.

2 Add the remaining ¹/₂-tablespoon oil, the garlic, and onion to the skillet. Sauté until the onion starts to soften, about 1 minute. Stir in the corn and cook 1 minute. Add the cherry tomatoes and cook 1 minute longer. Add the reserved shrimp and continue to sauté until they are opaque inside, 1–2 minutes. Remove from the heat and stir in the basil, salt, and pepper.

What's for Dinner

Serve the sauté warm over capellini pasta, or chilled over romaine lettuce as a main course salad.

COOK'S TIP Many markets now sell good quality, well-priced, frozen, precleaned uncooked shrimp, which you can use in place of fresh shrimp. Either thaw shrimp overnight in the refrigerator, or run under cold water for four to five minutes, until thawed. In a pinch, frozen corn also can be substituted for the fresh.

6 POINTS per serving

Per serving:
290 Calories • 12 g Total Fat • 2 g Saturated Fat • 172 mg Cholesterol • 471 mg Sodium • 23 g Total Carbohydrate
3 g Dietary Fiber • 26 g Protein • 80 mg Calcium

Blackened Tuna with Rémoulade Sauce

Makes 4 servings

1/2 cup reduced-fat mayonnaise

2 scallions, chopped

2 tablespoons chopped fresh parsley

4 teaspoons white vinegar

2 teaspoons capers, drained and chopped

2 teaspoons coarse-grained mustard

2 teaspoons paprika

1 1/2 teaspoons dried thyme

1 1/2 teaspoons dried oregano

1 tcaspoon garlic powder

1 teaspoon cayenne

1/2 teaspoon salt

4 (6-ounce) tuna steaks

2 teaspoons canola oil

Blackening, a well-known technique of Cajun cooking, was made popular when famed Louisiana chef Paul Prudhomme first fired up a skillet. This simple cooking method works well with almost any meaty fish, as well as with pork, chicken, and beef. It can generate a bit of smoke, however, so be prepared to turn on the exhaust or crack a window.

1 Combine the mayonnaise, scallions, parsley, vinegar, capers, and mustard in a bowl.

2 Mix together the paprika, thyme, oregano, garlic powder, cayenne, and salt in a small bowl. Sprinkle the mixture over both sides of each tuna steak.

3 Heat the oil in a large nonstick skillet until just starting to smoke. Add the tuna and cook until done, 2 minutes on each side for medium-rare. Serve the steaks with the sauce on the side.

What's for Dinner

Cool crunchy coleslaw tames the heat of blackened fish; make it with a vinegar, rather than a cream-style dressing. Serve with rustic-style mashed potatoes, made by roughly mashing cooked, unpeeled baking potato chunks with low-fat milk, salt, and coarsely ground black pepper.

8 POINTS per serving

Per serving:
348 Calories • 16 g Total Fat • 3 g Saturated Fat • 79 mg Cholesterol • 682 mg Sodium • 5 g Total Carbohydrate • 1 g Dietary Fiber • 43 g Protein • 49 mg Calcium

DINNER

Salad Bar Niçoise

The perfect salad bar meal! On your way home from work, stop by the market or deli with the largest and freshest selection of vegetables. Use the opportunity to try new veggies such as broccoli rabe, jicama, endive, exotic mushrooms, beet greens and others.

Makes 2 servings

1 (6-ounce) can solid white tuna in spring water, drained

4 cups assorted salad bar vegetables (such as cooked green beans, cherry tomatoes, baby carrots, sliced mushrooms, or sliced red onion)

6 kalamata or niçoise olives, pitted

$1/3$ cup fat-free Italian dressing

Mound the tuna in the center of a large serving plate. Arrange the vegetables around the tuna, scatter the olives over the top, and drizzle with the dressing.

What's for Dinner

All you'll need to finish this feast is a French baguette.

COOK'S TIP The key to transforming a recipe that's quick into a dish that's quick and delicious involves the simple addition of fresh herbs. Try mixing about two tablespoons of fresh basil slivers with the dressing.

Per serving:
192 Calories • 4 g Total Fat • 1 g Saturated Fat • 30 mg Cholesterol • 874 mg Sodium • 20 g Total Carbohydrate
6 g Dietary Fiber • 20 g Protein • 71 mg Calcium·

3 *POINTS* per serving

Chicken Marsala

This classic preparation also works nicely with veal. If you like, try shiitake or portobello mushrooms for a more intense, mushroom flavor.

Makes 4 servings

2 teaspoons olive oil

4 (4-ounce) thin-sliced skinless boneless chicken breasts

$1/2$ teaspoon salt

$1/2$ teaspoon coarsely ground black pepper

2 cups sliced mushrooms

2 teaspoons all-purpose flour

$1/4$ cup dry Marsala wine

$1/4$ cup reduced-sodium chicken broth

1 tablespoon chopped fresh parsley

1 Heat the oil in a large nonstick skillet over high heat. Sprinkle the chicken with salt and pepper. Add to the skillet and sauté until cooked through, about 3 minutes on each side. Transfer the chicken to a platter and cover to keep warm.

2 Add the mushrooms to the skillet; sauté until browned, about 3 minutes. Sprinkle the mushrooms with the flour, stirring to blend. Add the wine and broth; bring to a boil. Cook, stirring occasionally, until the sauce thickens, about 3 minutes longer. Stir in the parsley. Spoon the mushroom mixture over the chicken.

What's for Dinner

 The chicken is perfectly accented by wilted Swiss chard or kale and roasted potatoes.

COOK'S TIP If you can't find thin-sliced chicken breasts, buy skinless boneless chicken breasts. Place a breast between two sheets of waxed paper or plastic wrap, then lightly pound with a mallet or rolling pin.

Per serving:
164 Calories • 4 g Total Fat • 1 g Saturated Fat • 66 mg Cholesterol • 430 mg Sodium • 3 g Total Carbohydrate
0 g Dietary Fiber • 28 g Protein • 17 mg Calcium

4 POINTS per serving

DINNER

Polynesian Pineapple Chicken

Fresh ginger adds zest to this light, modern version of the restaurant classic, while snow peas and water chestnuts add crunch and texture. For a change, try shrimp or lean pork or beef instead of the chicken.

Makes 4 servings

1/3 cup ketchup

3 tablespoons reduced-sodium soy sauce

3 tablespoons sugar

2 tablespoons rice wine vinegar

1 tablespoon cornstarch

1 tablespoon canola oil

1 pound skinless boneless chicken breasts, cut into 1/2-inch cubes

1 tablespoon minced peeled fresh ginger

2 carrots, thinly sliced

1/2 pound snow peas, trimmed

1/4 cup slivered almonds

1 (8-ounce) can water chestnuts, drained

1 (8-ounce) can pineapple chunks in juice, drained

 1 Combine the ketchup, soy sauce, sugar, vinegar, and cornstarch in a bowl.

 2 Heat 2 teaspoons of the oil in a large nonstick skillet over medium-high heat. Add the chicken and cook, stirring occasionally, until cooked through, 5–6 minutes; remove from the skillet and reserve.

3 Add the remaining 1 teaspoon oil, ginger, and carrots to the skillet; cook, stirring occasionally, until the carrots begin to soften, about 2 minutes. Stir in the snow peas, almonds, water chestnuts, pineapple, and the reserved chicken. Cook, stirring often, 3–4 minutes. Add the ketchup mixture; bring to a boil and cook, stirring constantly, until thickened, about 1 minute.

What's for Dinner

Serve the chicken over quick-cooking brown rice or rice noodles.

 Because brown rice has a high-fiber bran coating, it goes rancid quickly and should only be stored for six months on the pantry shelf. It will last much longer if it is kept in the refrigerator.

Per serving:
363 Calories • 10 g Total Fat • 1 g Saturated Fat • 66 mg Cholesterol • 760 mg Sodium • 37 g Total Carbohydrate
6 g Dietary Fiber • 32 g Protein • 79 mg Calcium

Polynesian Pineapple Chicken

Chicken with Spicy Marmalade Glaze

Makes 4 servings

1/2 cup orange marmalade

2 scallions, chopped

1 tablespoon Dijon mustard

2 teaspoons fresh lemon juice

1/4 teaspoon crushed red pepper

4 (4-ounce) skinless boneless chicken breasts

1/2 teaspoon salt

Dijon mustard and crushed red pepper add some heat to the cool citrus marmalade used to glaze this attractive and zesty chicken dish. If you grill the chicken instead of broiling it, brush on the glaze only during the last minute or so of cooking to prevent it from burning.

1 Spray the rack of a broiler pan with nonstick spray; preheat the broiler.

2 Whisk together the marmalade, scallions, mustard, lemon juice, and crushed red pepper in a small bowl. Sprinkle both sides of the chicken with salt. Place the chicken on the broiler rack and brush with half of the marmalade mixture. Broil 3 inches from the heat, brushing periodically with the remaining glaze, until lightly browned, about 4 minutes on each side.

What's for Dinner

Serve with a medley of fresh or frozen cooked squash and green beans.

 COOK'S TIP This marmalade glaze also tastes fabulous on broiled or grilled pork chops.

5 POINTS per serving

Per serving:
245 Calories • 3 g Total Fat • 1 g Saturated Fat • 72 mg Cholesterol • 398 mg Sodium • 27 g Total Carbohydrate
2 g Dietary Fiber • 27 g Protein • 37 mg Calcium

Honey-Pecan Chicken

A crunchy coating of cornflakes and chopped pecans, flavored with just the right touch of honey, make this Southern-accented recipe one the whole family will love. This recipe also doubles as a main-dish salad: Simply cut the cooked chicken into strips and arrange on top of mixed greens tossed with light vinaigrette dressing.

Makes 4 servings

¹/₂ cup pecans

2 tablespoons cornflake crumbs

2 tablespoons honey

1 tablespoon reduced-sodium soy sauce

4 (5-ounce) skinless boneless chicken breasts

1 Preheat the oven to 425°F. Line a baking sheet with foil.

2 Finely chop the pecans in a food processor. Sprinkle the pecans and cornflake crumbs on a sheet of wax paper. Combine the honey and soy sauce in a shallow bowl. Dip both sides of each chicken breast into the honey mixture, then into the pecan mixture to coat. Arrange on the baking sheet in a single layer; spray lightly with nonstick spray. Bake until the chicken is cooked through, about 5 minutes on each side.

What's for Dinner

Pair the chicken with a tomato-cucumber salad and creamy mashed potatoes for a family feast.

COOK'S TIP A mini food processor is perfect for chopping a small amount of nuts.

---

7 POINTS per serving

Per serving:
296 Calories • 12 g Total Fat • 1 g Saturated Fat • 82 mg Cholesterol • 236 mg Sodium • 13 g Total Carbohydrate • 1 g Dietary Fiber • 35 g Protein • 26 mg Calcium

Chicken Tacos with Salsa Verde Cream

Children and grownups alike will enjoy this festive meal, which is a terrific way to use up leftover chicken. You can also try it with turkey, beef, or canned kidney beans (two 16-ounce cans). If you like, serve your favorite salsa on the side.

Makes 6 servings

²/3 cup light sour cream

2 tablespoons canned chopped mild green chiles, drained

2 tablespoons chopped fresh cilantro

¹/4 teaspoon salt

¹/4 teaspoon hot pepper sauce

12 corn taco shells, warmed

4 cups cooked cubed chicken breast

³/4 cup shredded reduced-fat sharp cheddar cheese

¹/2 cup shredded lettuce

2 tomatoes, seeded and chopped

Combine the sour cream, chiles, cilantro, salt, and pepper sauce in a small bowl. Fill the taco shells with equal amounts of the chicken, cheese, lettuce, and tomato; top each with 2 tablespoons of the sour cream mixture.

What's for Dinner

A salad of sliced grapefruit dressed with a touch of oil and vinegar provides a cool complement to the spicy tacos.

COOK'S TIP Warm the taco shells, wrapped in foil, in a toaster oven or a preheated 325° oven for three to four minutes.

8 POINTS per serving

Per serving:
374 Calories • 14 g Total Fat • 6 g Saturated Fat • 101 mg Cholesterol • 381 mg Sodium • 28 g Total Carbohydrate
3 g Dietary Fiber • 35 g Protein • 269 mg Calcium

Fennel-Crusted Flank Steak

An aromatic, crusty herb mixture makes a delicious topping for this lean flank steak. Try a ridged, nonstick grill pan to prepare this steak—it will look like it came off an outdoor grill. Be sure to let the steak rest for a few minutes before you slice it—slicing right out of the pan causes the juices to run, making the meat dry.

Makes 4 servings

1 tablespoon fennel seeds, crushed

1 teaspoon chopped fresh thyme

1 teaspoon chopped fresh rosemary

1 garlic clove, minced

1 teaspoon salt

1/2 teaspoon coarsely ground black pepper

1 (1-pound) flank steak, trimmed of all visible fat

1 Combine the fennel, thyme, rosemary, garlic, salt, and pepper in a small bowl.

2 Heat a large nonstick skillet or ridged grill pan over high heat. Meanwhile, rub the fennel mixture onto both sides of the steak. Put the steak in the skillet and sear until browned, 4–5 minutes. Turn the steak over and cook until done to taste, about 5 minutes longer for medium. Transfer the steak to a cutting board; let stand 5 minutes. Thinly slice steak on the diagonal against the grain.

What's for Dinner

Yolkless egg noodles and cooked cabbage pair well with this steak.

COOK'S TIP The quickest and easiest way to crush fennel seeds is in a spice or coffee grinder. You could also use a mortar and pestle, or sprinkle the seeds onto a towel and crush them with a mallet or a heavy, flat-bottomed mug or jar.

Per serving:
206 Calories • 8 g Total Fat • 3 g Saturated Fat • 49 mg Cholesterol • 632 mg Sodium • 1 g Total Carbohydrate
1 g Dietary Fiber • 30 g Protein • 26 mg Calcium

5 *POINTS* per serving

Turkey Rolls Cordon Bleu

Breaded cutlet dishes are an all-time favorite, but the traditional preparation of coating in flour, egg, and crumbs is high in calories, messy, and labor intensive. We simplify the breading process by brushing the cutlets lightly with reduced-calorie mayonnaise, then dipping them in crumbs—it works well with chicken and fish too. If you like your cutlets a bit on the spicy side, brush them with mustard instead of mayonnaise or a combination of the two.

Makes 4 servings

4¼ pound turkey cutlets raw

4 (1-ounce) slices reduced-sodium ham

2 (1-ounce) slices reduced-fat Swiss cheese, halved

3 tablespoons plain dry bread crumbs

1 tablespoon reduced-calorie mayonnaise

¼ cup dry white wine

¼ cup reduced-sodium chicken broth

1 teaspoon butter

 Top each cutlet with a slice of ham and then a half slice of cheese. Roll up jelly-roll fashion and secure with toothpicks.

 Spread the bread crumbs on a plate or a sheet of wax paper. Brush the turkey rolls with mayonnaise; dip in the crumbs, pressing down to coat.

 Spray a large nonstick skillet with nonstick spray and set over medium-high heat. Add the turkey rolls and sauté until browned all over, about 5 minutes. Add the wine, broth, and butter; bring to a boil. Cover, reduce the heat, and simmer until the turkey is cooked through and the sauce thickens, about 5 minutes longer.

What's for Dinner

 Simple steamed baby broccoli and a simple linguine with herbs make terrific accompaniments to the rich turkey rolls.

COOK'S TIP If substituting skinless boneless chicken breasts for the turkey cutlets, you may want to pound them so they're thin enough to roll up easily. You can also substitute an equal amount of chicken broth for the white wine.

Per serving:
234 Calories • 6 g Total Fat • 3 g Saturated Fat • 95 mg Cholesterol • 434 mg Sodium • 5 g Total Carbohydrate
0 g Dietary Fiber • 37 g Protein • 125 mg Calcium

5 POINTS per serving

Turkey Rolls Cordon Bleu

DINNER

Steak with Spicy Chili Sauce

Red chili paste, one of the countless robust Thai sauces that can now be found in the Asian section of most supermarkets, is the basis for a luscious sauce. It gives the steak a rich flavor, as well as deep mahogany color. Look for tenderloins that are about one-inch thick.

Makes 4 servings

¹/₂ cup red wine vinegar

3 tablespoons packed light brown sugar

2 shallots, minced

1 tablespoon Thai red chili paste

1 garlic clove, minced

1¹/₂ teaspoons vegetable oil

³/₄ teaspoon salt

4 (4-ounce) beef tenderloin steaks

1 Combine the vinegar, brown sugar, shallots, chili paste, garlic, 1 teaspoon of the oil, and ¹/₄ teaspoon of the salt in a bowl. Add the steaks, turning to coat evenly. Remove the steaks, reserving the sauce; pat the steaks lightly with paper towels and sprinkle with remaining ¹/₂ teaspoon salt.

2 Heat the remaining ¹/₂ teaspoon oil in a large nonstick skillet over high heat until almost smoking. Arrange the steaks in a single layer so that they don't touch. Cook until done to taste, 4 minutes on each side for medium-rare. Transfer the steaks to a plate and cover to keep warm.

3 Add the reserved sauce to the pan. Bring to a boil over medium-high heat and cook, stirring occasionally, until thick and syrupy, about 3 minutes. Spoon the sauce over steaks.

What's for Dinner

Serve with stir-fried snow peas and oven baked "fries."

6 POINTS per serving

Per serving:
234 Calories • 10 g Total Fat • 3 g Saturated Fat • 57 mg Cholesterol • 600 mg Sodium • 12 g Total Carbohydrate
0 g Dietary Fiber • 24 g Protein • 19 mg Calcium

Beef and Vegetable Salad with Pickled Ginger Dressing

This no-cook, main-dish Asian salad is perfect for those days when you're heading home from work exhausted and hungry. A quick stop at your supermarket's deli counter and a stroll through the produce department will provide almost all the ingredients.

*Makes 4 servings
(yield 6 cups)*

$^1/_2$ pound lean deli-sliced roast beef

2 cups halved mushrooms

1 cup sugar snap peas or snow peas, trimmed

1 cup halved baby carrots

6 scallions, sliced

1 red bell pepper, seeded and sliced

$^1/_4$ cup seasoned rice vinegar

1 tablespoon reduced-sodium soy sauce

1 tablespoon pickled ginger, drained and finely chopped

1 tablespoon Asian (dark) sesame oil

Combine the roast beef, mushrooms, sugar snap peas, carrots, scallions, and bell pepper in a large bowl. Whisk together the vinegar, soy sauce, ginger, and oil in a small bowl. Spoon the dressing over the salad and stir to coat.

What's for Dinner

Serve the salad with crunchy rice crackers or pick up whole-wheat French bread while you are in the supermarket.

COOK'S TIP Pickled ginger is thinly sliced, light pink in color, and slightly sweet from being preserved in sweet vinegar. It can be found in jars in the Asian section of your supermarket or in Asian markets.

Per serving:
215 Calories • 6 g Total Fat • 2 g Saturated Fat • 39 mg Cholesterol • 689 mg Sodium • 19 g Total Carbohydrate
4 g Dietary Fiber • 20 g Protein • 56 mg Calcium

4 POINTS per serving

Veal Picatta

This classic veal preparation has been a favorite in Italian restaurants for decades. In the market, look for veal scaloppine, which are thin cutlets. If you don't see any prepackaged, ask the butcher to prepare them for you.

Makes 4 servings

1 1/2 cups quick-cooking rice

2 tablespoons all-purpose flour

3/4 teaspoon salt

1/4 teaspoon coarsely ground black pepper

1 pound veal scaloppine (from top round leg)

2 tablespoons butter

1/3 cup fresh lemon juice

1/3 cup dry white wine

1 tablespoon capers, drained

1 Prepare the rice according to package directions, omitting the addition of any fat.

2 Combine the flour, 1/4 teaspoon of the salt, and 1/8 teaspoon of the pepper in a shallow bowl. Dip the veal in the flour mixture to coat.

3 Melt 1 tablespoon of the butter in a large nonstick skillet over medium-high heat. Add the veal and cook until browned, 2–3 minutes on each side. Reduce the heat to medium and add the lemon juice, wine, and capers. Cook 1 minute longer, turning the cutlets once to coat with sauce. Remove the pan from the heat and transfer the veal to a plate. Stir the remaining 1 tablespoon butter, 1/2 teaspoon salt, and 1/8 teaspoon pepper into the pan, swirling until the butter melts. Serve the veal and sauce over the rice.

What's for Dinner

 Sliced zucchini with tomatoes makes an authentic— and terrific—accompaniment.

 COOK'S TIP
Slice the zucchini in a food processor that has been fitted with a fine slicing disk. Place the zucchini slices and a can of drained, chopped Italian-style tomatoes in a small saucepan and cook over a low heat until the zucchini is tender. You also can substitute an equal amount of water for the alcohol.

Per serving:
338 Calories • 8 g Total Fat • 4 g Saturated Fat • 105 mg Cholesterol • 648 mg Sodium • 36 g Total Carbohydrate
1 g Dietary Fiber • 28 g Protein • 12 mg Calcium

7 POINTS per serving

Rosemary-Mustard Lamb Steaks

Rosemary and lamb are a delicious and elegant pairing. If time allows, use two tablespoons chopped fresh rosemary instead of dried in the rub; cover the steaks and let them sit in the refrigerator for one hour to allow the flavors to meld.

Makes 4 servings

2 tablespoons Dijon mustard

2 teaspoons dried rosemary, crumbled

2 garlic cloves, minced

1/2 teaspoon salt

1/4 teaspoon coarsely ground black pepper

2 (8-ounce) leg lamb steaks, trimmed of all visible fat

1 Preheat the broiler.

2 Combine the mustard, rosemary, garlic, salt, and pepper in a bowl. Rub the mixture over the steaks to coat.

3 Broil the steaks 4 inches from the heat until an instant-read thermometer inserted in the thickest part of the lamb steak reads 145°F for medium-rare or 160°F for medium, about 4–5 minutes on each side for medium-rare. Cut each steak in half.

What's for Dinner

Perfect in the spring, served with boiled new potatoes and steamed fresh baby vegetables, or during the winter months with instant mashed potatoes and steamed broccoli.

 COOK'S TIP Prepare instant mashed potatoes with low-fat milk and season with salt and coarsely ground black pepper.

3 POINTS per serving

Per serving:
129 Calories • 6 g Total Fat • 2 g Saturated Fat • 52 mg Cholesterol • 374 mg Sodium • 2 g Total Carbohydrate
0 g Dietary Fiber • 17 g Protein • 25 mg Calcium

Garlicky Seared Lamb Chops with Mint Vinaigrette

Lamb chops are a special occasion treat at any time of year. In the summer, when there's an abundant supply of fresh mint, you can serve them with this wonderful vinaigrette.

Makes 4 servings

3 tablespoons from 1 (14^1/$_2$-ounce) can reduced-sodium chicken broth (reserve the remaining broth to cook the couscous to serve with the chops)

1 tablespoon olive oil

1 shallot, minced

1 garlic clove, minced

1 tablespoon grated lemon zest

1 tablespoon fresh lemon juice

^{1}/$_4$ cup chopped fresh mint

1 teaspoon dried oregano

^{3}/$_4$ teaspoon salt

4 (4-ounce) loin or rib-eye lamb chops, trimmed of all visible fat

^{1}/$_2$ teaspoon coarsely ground black pepper

 Combine the broth, oil, shallot, garlic, lemon zest, lemon juice, mint, oregano, and ^{1}/$_4$ teaspoon of the salt in a bowl.

 Sprinkle both sides of the lamb chops with the remaining ^{1}/$_2$-teaspoon salt and the pepper.

 Preheat a large nonstick skillet over high heat. Spray with nonstick spray. Put the lamb chops into the skillet and cook until crusty, browned, and done to taste, about 3 minutes on each side for medium-rare. Transfer the chops to a platter. Stir and spoon the mint vinaigrette over the meat.

What's for Dinner

Serve the lamb chops with couscous cooked in the remainder of the can of reduced-sodium chicken broth, along with cooked tiny peas on the side.

 COOK'S TIP The best way to produce a crusty piece of meat or fish when pan-searing it is to make sure the meat is perfectly dry and the heat relatively high; any moisture on the meat will generate steam, and insufficient heat will not produce a good crust.

5 *POINTS* per serving

Per serving:
229 Calories • 12 g Total Fat • 3 g Saturated Fat • 81 mg Cholesterol • 536 mg Sodium • 3 g Total Carbohydrate
1 g Dietary Fiber • 26 g Protein • 42 mg Calcium

Garlicky Seared Lamb Chops with Mint Vinaigrette

Three-Cheesy Pizza

Americans do love pizza and we've finally learned that less is definitely more as far as toppings are concerned. Our version boasts a triad of cheeses: part-skim ricotta, mozzarella, and a bit of grated Parmesan.

Makes 4 servings

3/4 cup part-skim ricotta cheese

1 (10-ounce) prebaked pizza crust

4 ounces fat-free sliced ham, coarsely chopped

3/4 cup shredded part-skim mozzarella cheese

2 tablespoons grated Parmesan cheese

1 Preheat the oven to 450°F.

2 Spread the ricotta evenly over the pizza crust. Top with the ham, mozzarella, and Parmesan cheese.

3 Place the pizza on an ungreased baking sheet and bake until the crust is crisp and the cheese has melted, 8–10 minutes.

What's for Dinner

 Fresh arugula salad gives a peppery contrast to this mellow pizza.

 COOK'S TIP For a little green in your pizza, scatter one cup of chopped fresh spinach over the pizza crust with the ham.

7 POINTS per serving

Per serving:
304 Calories • 11 g Total Fat • 5 g Saturated Fat • 42 mg Cholesterol • 833 mg Sodium • 29 g Total Carbohydrate
0 g Dietary Fiber • 22 g Protein • 382 mg Calcium

Pork Medallions with Ginger Pears and Chutney

Pork tenderloin is a healthy cook's dream; it's lean and low in fat, and ready to cook with little prepping. We pair it with a sophisticated, ginger-spiked chutney. Use ripe, but firm, Bosc or Anjou pears, which will hold up well during cooking.

Makes 4 servings

3/4 pound pork tenderloin, cut into 1-inch slices

1/2 teaspoon salt

1/2 teaspoon coarsely ground black pepper

2 teaspoons canola oil

2 pears, peeled, cored, and cut into chunks

2 teaspoons grated peeled fresh ginger

1 garlic clove, minced

1/4 cup mango chutney

1/4 cup reduced-sodium chicken broth

2 teaspoons chopped fresh thyme, or 1/2 teaspoon dried

1 Sprinkle the pork with salt and pepper. Heat 1 teaspoon of the oil in a nonstick skillet over high heat. Arrange the pork in the skillet in a single layer so that the slices don't touch, in batches if necessary; cook until browned, about 3 minutes on each side. Transfer the meat to a plate and cover to keep warm.

2 Add the remaining 1 teaspoon oil to the skillet. Add the pears, ginger, and garlic. Cook, stirring often, until the pears are tender and golden, about 5 minutes. Add the chutney, broth, and thyme. Bring to a boil, scraping the browned bits from the bottom of the skillet, and cook until the sauce thickens slightly, about 5 minutes.

3 Arrange the pork on a platter and spoon the pear mixture on top.

What's for Dinner

 Serve with roasted new potatoes and sautéed bok choy.

4 POINTS per serving   **Per serving:**
201 Calories • 6 g Total Fat • 1 g Saturated Fat • 54 mg Cholesterol • 411 mg Sodium • 18 g Total Carbohydrate
2 g Dietary Fiber • 19 g Protein • 29 mg Calcium

Pork Medallions with Port and Plums

Makes 4 servings

1 teaspoon canola oil

1 onion, thinly sliced

2 plums (purple or red), cut into $1/4$-inch wedges

1 $1/2$ pounds pork tenderloin, cut into 1 $1/2$-inch slices and pounded to $1/4$-inch thick

$1/2$ cup port wine

2 tablespoons fresh lime juice

2 tablespoons sugar

$3/4$ teaspoon salt

$1/4$ teaspoon coarsely ground black pepper

$1/8$ teaspoon ground cinnamon

1 tablespoon chopped fresh cilantro

Port, a fortified Portuguese wine, has a rich mellow flavor that adds just the right depth of taste to countless sauces and desserts. This intensely flavored sauce also makes an excellent accompaniment to grilled or sautéed duck breasts. The cilantro is an unexpectedly delicious accent that adds intrigue.

Heat the oil in a large nonstick skillet over medium-high heat. Add the onion and cook, stirring occasionally, until it begins to soften, about 2 minutes. Add the plums and pork. Cook 4 minutes and turn the pork medallions over. Stir in the port, lime juice, sugar, salt, pepper, and cinnamon. Cover, reduce the heat to medium, and simmer until the pork is cooked through, about 4 minutes longer. Remove from the heat and stir in the cilantro.

What's for Dinner

Serve the pork with quick-cooking white or brown rice and a frozen vegetable combination.

 COOK'S TIP If you don't have a meat tenderizer, pound the pork with a rubber mallet or a rolling pin.

7 POINTS per serving

Per serving:
300 Calories • 9 g Total Fat • 3 g Saturated Fat • 107 mg Cholesterol • 525 mg Sodium • 16 g Total Carbohydrate
1 g Dietary Fiber • 37 g Protein • 34 mg Calcium

Pineapple Pork Sauté

There is an array of tasty low-fat bottled sauces now available in most supermarkets (often in the Asian section). In this recipe, you can substitute a teriyaki sauce for the sweet and sour variety, however, omit the salt if you do.

Makes 3 servings

1 cup quick-cooking brown rice

3/4 pound pork tenderloin, thinly sliced against the grain

3/4 teaspoon salt

1/2 teaspoon coarsely ground black pepper

1 teaspoon vegetable oil

3 scallions, sliced on the diagonal into 2-inch pieces

1 small apple, peeled, cored, and chopped

1 red bell pepper, seeded and chopped

1 garlic clove, chopped

1/4 teaspoon crushed red pepper

1 (8-ounce can) pineapple chunks in juice, drained

1/2 cup Chinese-style sweet and sour sauce

 Cook the rice according to package directions.

 Sprinkle the pork with the salt and pepper. Spray a large nonstick skillet with nonstick spray and set over medium-high heat. Arrange the pork in the skillet in a single layer, cooking in batches if necessary. Sauté until browned and cooked through, 1–2 minutes on each side. Transfer the pork to a plate.

3 Add the oil to the skillet. Stir in the scallions, apple, bell pepper, garlic, and crushed red pepper. Sauté until tender, about 5 minutes. Stir in the pineapple, sauce, and reserved pork; bring to a boil. Serve with rice.

What's for Dinner

Serve with steamed greens, such as spinach, and drained, canned Mandarin orange slices.

COOK'S TIP It's a bit more expensive, but consider substituting 1 cup fresh pineapple cubes for the canned. Thanks to the prepackaged fresh pineapple now found in the produce section of your supermarket, it isn't labor intensive to prepare.

8 POINTS per serving

Per serving:
407 Calories • 6 g Total Fat • 1 g Saturated Fat • 67 mg Cholesterol • 784 mg Sodium • 58 g Total Carbohydrate
4 g Dietary Fiber • 31 g Protein • 48 mg Calcium

DINNER

Hoisin Pork Stir-Fry

Once the ingredients are prepped, this stir-fry is a cinch—the meal is done in minutes. Be sure to use lean pork tenderloin, top loin, or sirloin—other varieties of precut pork are from fattier cuts of meat.

Makes 4 servings (yield 4 cups + 2 cups rice)

1$^1/_2$ cups quick-cooking rice

$^3/_4$ pound boneless pork loin, trimmed of all visible fat and cut into strips for stir-fry

2 tablespoons dry sherry

1 tablespoon reduced-sodium soy sauce

1 tablespoon cornstarch

1 teaspoon Asian (dark) sesame oil

2 cups broccoli florets

1 red bell pepper, seeded and chopped

$^1/_4$ cup orange juice

$^1/_4$ cup hoisin sauce

2 tablespoons honey

1 Cook the rice according to package directions, omitting the addition of any fat.

2 Combine the pork, sherry, soy sauce, and cornstarch in a bowl.

3 Heat the oil in a large nonstick skillet over medium–high heat until nearly smoking. Add the broccoli and red pepper and stir-fry 2 minutes. Add the pork strips and stir-fry 4 minutes. Add the orange juice, hoisin, and honey; cook until the pork is cooked through, about 2 minutes longer. Serve over the rice.

What's for Dinner

 A sliced cucumber salad, either homemade or from your favorite deli counter, will set this stir-fry off in style.

 COOK'S TIP To make your own simple, tasty cucumber salad, pull out your food processor to mince one small red onion. Transfer the onion to a bowl, then fit the processor with a fine slicing disk and slice two large peeled cucumbers. Add to the onion and drizzle with oil and vinegar.

Per serving (1 cup and $^1/_2$ cup rice):
313 Calories • 6 g Total Fat • 2 g Saturated Fat • 54 mg Cholesterol • 453 mg Sodium • 43 g Total Carbohydrate
3 g Dietary Fiber • 22 g Protein • 51 mg Calcium

6 *POINTS* per serving

Roast Pork, Orange, and Beet Salad

The flavors in this salad hail from Mexico. The combination might sound unusual, but it is delectable. Although jarred beets work fine, roasted beets are superb. On a night when you have the time, wrap two or three trimmed small beets in foil and roast in a 400–425°F oven until tender (about an hour); cool slightly, then peel and slice.

Makes 4 servings

2 tablespoons red-wine vinegar

2 teaspoons vegetable oil

$^1/_2$ teaspoon salt

4 cups torn romaine lettuce

2 cups thinly sliced lean roasted pork loin

2 oranges, peeled and thinly sliced

1 red onion, thinly sliced

2 tablespoons minced cilantro

$^1/_2$ jalapeño pepper, seeded, deveined, and minced (wear gloves to prevent irritation)

1 cup sliced cooked beets

1 Whisk the vinegar, oil, and salt in a small bowl.

2 Combine the lettuce, pork, oranges, onion, cilantro, and jalapeño in a bowl. Drizzle with the dressing and toss to combine.

3 Divide the beets among 4 salad plates; top with the salad.

What's for Dinner

 For a pleasant, light dinner, serve with a crusty baguette and a glass of wine.

3 POINTS per serving

Per serving:
187 Calories • 6 g Total Fat • 2 g Saturated Fat • 46 mg Cholesterol • 338 mg Sodium • 14 g Total Carbohydrate
4 g Dietary Fiber • 18 g Protein • 63 mg Calcium

20 minute recipes

BREAKFAST

LUNCH

BREAKFAST

Blueberry-Lemon Cornmeal Pancakes

Cornmeal lends an unexpected crunch to these citrus-scented berry pancakes. For added flavor substitute an equal amount of maple syrup or honey for the sugar in the batter.

Makes 4 servings
(yield 12 pancakes)

1 cup reduced-fat
all-purpose baking mix

1 cup yellow cornmeal

1¼ cups low-fat
(1%) milk

1 large egg, lightly beaten

3 tablespoons sugar

1 tablespoon grated
lemon zest

¼ teaspoon ground ginger

1 cup fresh or frozen
blueberries

1 Combine the baking mix, cornmeal, milk, egg, sugar, lemon zest, and ginger in a bowl. Gently stir in the blueberries.

2 Heat a nonstick griddle or skillet over medium heat. Spray with non-stick spray. Using heaping ¼ cupfuls for each pancake, pour the batter onto the griddle. Cook until bubbles begin to appear around the edges of the pancakes, 2–3 minutes. Turn the pancakes and cook until golden, about 2 minutes longer. Keep warm until ready to serve.

What's for Breakfast

Ham steaks complement these pancakes nicely. For a special touch, combine raspberries, blueberries, and sliced strawberries with a little maple syrup for a topping.

COOK'S TIP If using frozen—rather than fresh—blueberries, do not thaw, or the berries will become too mushy.

6 POINTS per serving

Per serving:
341 Calories • 5 g Total Fat • 2 g Saturated Fat • 56 mg Cholesterol • 388 mg Sodium • 64 mg Total Carbohydrate
4 g Dietary Fiber • 10 g Protein • 136 mg Calcium

Tangy Yogurt Pancakes with Blueberry Compote

Makes 4 servings (yield 12 pancakes and 3/4 cup compote)

1 cup fresh or frozen blueberries

6 tablespoons sugar

2 tablespoons fresh lemon juice

1 tablespoon water

1 1/3 cups all-purpose flour

1 teaspoon baking powder

1/4 teaspoon baking soda

1/4 teaspoon salt

1/8 teaspoon ground nutmeg

1 (8-ounce) container plain nonfat yogurt (about 3/4 cup)

1/2 cup fat-free milk

1 large egg

1 tablespoon canola oil

1/2 teaspoon vanilla extract

Nonfat yogurt gives these pancakes a light and fluffy texture, as well as a distinctively tangy flavor that is perfectly complemented by the sweet blueberry compote. Try this sophisticated alternative to everyday pancakes and syrup for your next breakfast or brunch. Serve the pancakes immediately or keep them warm in a 250°F oven until ready to serve.

 Combine the blueberries, 4 tablespoons of the sugar, lemon juice, and water in a small saucepan. Bring to a boil over medium-high heat; reduce the heat and simmer, stirring occasionally, until slightly thickened, about 12 minutes. Remove from the heat and keep warm.

2 Meanwhile, combine the flour, the remaining 2 tablespoons sugar, baking powder, baking soda, salt, and nutmeg in a bowl. In a separate bowl, combine the yogurt, milk, egg, oil, and vanilla. Add the flour mixture to the yogurt mixture, stirring just until smooth.

3 Heat a nonstick skillet or nonstick griddle over medium heat. Using a scant 1/4 cup for each pancake, pour the batter into the pan. Cook just until the tops are covered with bubbles and the edges are cooked, 2–3 minutes. Turn the pancakes and cook until browned, about 2 minutes more. Serve with the warm blueberry compote.

What's for Breakfast

 Crisp-cooked slices of turkey bacon add texture and flavor to compliment the pancakes and compote.

---

7 POINTS per serving

Per serving (3 pancakes and 3 tablespoons compote):
337 Calories • 5 g Total Fat • 1 g Saturated Fat • 55 mg Cholesterol • 401 mg Sodium • 62 mg Total Carbohydrate 2 g Dietary Fiber • 10 g Protein • 1,835 mg Calcium

Brown Rice Congee with Milk and Butter

Makes 6 servings
(yield 3 cups)

2 cups quick-cooking
brown rice

1/2 cup fat-free milk

3 tablespoons sugar

1 teaspoon vanilla extract

1 tablespoon butter

In China, congee is a porridge of rice and water that is often served as a savory dish. It also is popular as a breakfast dish, and is a nice change of pace from more typical breakfast cereals. When cooking, add a little extra water if you prefer your porridge less thick.

Cook the rice according to package directions, using about 1/4 cup more water than called for. Stir in the milk, sugar, and vanilla and cook 1 minute over low heat. Remove from the heat and stir in the butter.

What's for Breakfast

This nutritious breakfast is made complete with fresh seasonal fruit and multi-grain toast spread with peanut butter.

3 POINTS per serving

Per serving:
150 Calories • 3 g Total Fat • 1 g Saturated Fat • 6 mg Cholesterol • 35 mg Sodium • 29 mg Total Carbohydrate
1 g Dietary Fiber • 3 g Protein • 39 mg Calcium

Western Omelet

Also known as a Denver omelet, this classic combination of onion, green pepper, and ham in a fluffy egg mixture can be served for lunch, brunch, or late night supper. You can even serve the omelet inside a toasted bun or between slices of toast. If you like your eggs spicy, add some sliced jalapeño or other hot pepper (wear gloves to prevent irritation when seeding and slicing the pepper) or a few drops of hot pepper sauce.

Makes 2 servings

1 teaspoon butter

$1/4$ cup chopped onion

$1/4$ cup seeded and chopped green bell pepper

$1/4$ pound deli-sliced ham, chopped

$1/4$ teaspoon dried thyme

$1/8$ teaspoon coarsely ground black pepper

1 cup fat-free egg substitute

Melt the butter in a nonstick skillet over medium heat. Add the onion, bell pepper, ham, thyme, and black pepper. Cook, stirring occasionally, until the vegetables soften, 4–5 minutes. Pour in the egg substitute and swirl to cover the pan; cook, stirring gently, until the underside begins to set, about 3 minutes. Fold one side of the omelet over the other and cook 2 minutes. Flip and cook until cooked through, about 1 minute longer.

What's for Breakfast

Get the day off to a good start and serve your omelet with cornmeal scones or corn muffins and your favorite fresh fruit.

 COOK'S TIP For best results when making an omelet, use a heavy nonstick skillet with curved sides, so that the omelet will easily slide onto a plate.

4 POINTS per serving

Per serving:
179 Calories • 5 g Total Fat • 2 g Saturated Fat • 37 mg Cholesterol • 974 mg Sodium • 5 mg Total Carbohydrate
1 g Dietary Fiber • 27g Protein • 50 mg Calcium

Turkey Hash Patties

A wonderful alternative to fatty sausage patties or bacon, these lean turkey patties are made hash-style with potato and onion. You can top them with a little chili sauce, just as you would hash.

Makes 6 servings

1 medium-large baking potato, peeled

1 onion, peeled

¹/2 pound ground turkey breast

1 large egg white

1 tablespoon Worcestershire sauce

³/4 teaspoon salt

¹/2 teaspoon coarsely ground black pepper

¹/2 teaspoon ground sage

2 teaspoons canola oil

1 Grate the potato and onion into a large bowl. Stir in the turkey, egg white, Worcestershire sauce, salt, pepper, and sage. Shape into eighteen 3-inch round patties.

2 Heat the oil in a large nonstick skillet over medium-high heat. Add the patties in one layer and cook, in batches, until browned, about 4 minutes on each side.

What's for Breakfast

Make an English-style "fry-up" and serve these patties with fried, poached, or scrambled eggs and fried tomato halves.

 COOK'S TIP To fry tomatoes, place tomato halves, cut-side down in the same skillet as you cooked the turkey patties and cook over medium-high heat until browned and heated through, about three minutes.

2 POINTS per serving

Per serving:
95 Calories • 2 g Total Fat • 0 g Saturated Fat • 20 mg Cholesterol • 348 mg Sodium • 8 mg Total Carbohydrate
1 g Dietary Fiber • 10 g Protein • 16 mg Calcium

Tomato, White Bean, and Arugula Bruschetta

Makes 4 servings (yield 2 cups bean mixture)

1 (15¹/2-ounce) can white kidney or cannellini beans, rinsed and drained

1 tomato, seeded and chopped

¹/2 cup finely chopped arugula

2 teaspoons balsamic vinegar

2 teaspoons extra-virgin olive oil

1 teaspoon grated lemon zest

¹/2 teaspoon dried oregano

8 ounces French bread (about ¹/2 baguette), cut into twelve ¹/2-inch slices

1 large garlic clove, peeled

For an easy but elegant lunch, set out a tray of this flavorful, light bruschetta. It's also a perfect party food that holds up well on the buffet—a great hors d'oeuvre that requires little in the way of fuss, yet will elicit rave reviews from your guests. The bean mixture, without the arugula, can be made up to two days ahead. Store it in the refrigerator then stir in the arugula at the last minute.

 1 Put one-half of the beans in a bowl and mash with a fork. Stir in the remaining beans, the tomato, arugula, vinegar, oil, lemon zest, and oregano; mix well.

2 Toast the bread until crisp. Rub one side of each slice with the garlic; top with bean mixture.

What's for Lunch

 Try serving the bruschetta with a mixture of sliced, fresh fennel, red bell pepper strips, and little balls of fresh mozzarella cheese.

 COOK'S TIP Spear the garlic clove with the tines of a fork to rub it easily over the bread.

Per serving:
252 Calories • 5 g Total Fat • 1 g Saturated Fat • 0 mg Cholesterol • 570 mg Sodium • 47 mg Total Carbohydrate
7 g Dietary Fiber • 11 g Protein • 102 mg Calcium

5 *POINTS* per serving

LUNCH

Black Bean Nachos with Jicama Salsa

Jicama, with its apple-like texture and slightly sweet flavor, lends an interesting touch to these guilt-free nachos. The salsa is so easy to make you can whip it up for a quick snack whenever you have the yen.

Makes 4 servings (yield about 3 cups salsa)

1/4 pound baked fat-free tortilla chips

1 cup canned black beans, rinsed and drained

1/2 cup shredded reduced-fat cheddar cheese

1 1/2 cups chopped jicama

1 tomato, seeded and chopped

1 small red onion, diced

8 pitted black olives, thinly sliced

3 tablespoons pickled jalapeño slices, drained

3 tablespoons fresh lime juice

2 tablespoons chopped cilantro

1/2 teaspoon salt

 1 Preheat the oven to 425°F. Spread the tortilla chips on a baking sheet and top with the beans and the cheese. Bake until the cheese melts, 4–5 minutes.

2 Meanwhile, combine the jicama, tomato, onion, olives, jalapeño slices, lime juice, cilantro, and salt in a bowl. Carefully transfer the nachos to a platter and spoon on the jicama salsa.

What's for Lunch

For a heartier meal, add some shredded, cooked chicken with the beans and cheese.

4 POINTS **per serving**

Per serving:
230 Calories • 5 g Total Fat • 2 g Saturated Fat • 8 mg Cholesterol • 899 mg Sodium • 41 mg Total Carbohydrate
9 g Dietary Fiber • 11 g Protein • 249 mg Calcium

Texas Black-Eyed Pea Salad

Black-eyed peas are a favorite throughout the South and the basis of Hoppin' John, a Southern New Year's Eve delicacy believed to bring good luck in the coming year. It can be served as a side dish, as well as for lunch. If your schedule allows, make the salad ahead of time, cover, and let the flavors meld for 30 minutes at room temperature or two hours in the refrigerator.

*Makes 6 servings
(yield 6 cups)*

1 (15-ounce) can black-eyed peas, rinsed and drained

6 scallions, chopped

3 plum tomatoes, chopped

2 celery stalks, chopped

1 green bell pepper, seeded and chopped

1 red bell pepper, seeded and chopped

2 tablespoons chopped cilantro

1 teaspoon grated lime zest

2 tablespoons fresh lime juice

2 tablespoons cider vinegar

2 tablespoons canola oil

2 teaspoons sugar

$1/2$ teaspoon salt

$1/2$ teaspoon coarsely ground black pepper

Combine the black-eyed peas, scallions, tomatoes, celery, bell peppers, cilantro, lime zest, lime juice, vinegar, oil, sugar, salt, and black pepper in a large bowl; mix well.

What's for Lunch

Grill turkey or chicken sausage and serve it with the salad for a substantial and satisfying meal.

 COOK'S TIP For vegetarians, Hoppin' John can be served with cooked rice, which teams well with the black-eyed peas to make a complete protein.

2 POINTS per serving

Per serving:
126 Calories • 5 g Total Fat • 0 g Saturated Fat • 0 mg Cholesterol • 298 mg Sodium • 17 mg Total Carbohydrate
4 g Dietary Fiber • 5 g Protein • 47 mg Calcium

Portobello Burgers

Portobello mushrooms with their rich flavor and texture, make a terrific low-fat substitute for burgers. English muffins are just the right size and shape to hold these burgers.

Makes 4 servings

4 portobello mushrooms, stemmed

2 tablespoons olive oil

$^1/_2$ teaspoon salt

$^1/_4$ teaspoon coarsely ground black pepper

2 garlic cloves, minced

1 teaspoon dried oregano

1 teaspoon dried basil

$^1/_4$ cup balsamic vinegar

4 English muffins, split and toasted

2 tablespoons Dijon mustard

4 lettuce leaves

4 slices tomato

1 Brush the mushrooms with 2 teaspoons of the oil and sprinkle with the salt and pepper. Heat 2 teaspoons of the oil in a large nonstick skillet over medium-high heat. Add the mushrooms, cover, and cook until browned and tender, about 6 minutes on each side. Transfer to a plate and cover to keep warm.

2 To the skillet, add the remaining 2 teaspoons oil, the garlic, oregano, and basil; cook 30 seconds. Add the vinegar and cook until slightly syrupy, about 2 minutes. Add the mushrooms and turn to coat.

3 Spread a half of each muffin with 1$^1/_2$ teaspoons of the mustard; layer with a lettuce leaf, a tomato slice, and a mushroom. Brush with any remaining syrup from the skillet. Cover with the remaining muffin halves.

What's for Lunch

Portobello burgers are lean enough to allow for an indulgence—serve with some blue cheese and fresh pear slices.

5 *POINTS* per serving

Per serving:
256 Calories • 8 g Total Fat • 1 g Saturated Fat • 0 mg Cholesterol • 601 mg Sodium • 35 mg Total Carbohydrate
6 g Dietary Fiber • 9 g Protein • 178 mg Calcium

Greek Pita Pizzas

The flavors of the Mediterranean make this simple entrée a great lunch or late weeknight dinner. Like any dish that calls for fresh tomato, its taste will be exceptional if you make it during the months when vine-ripened tomatoes are plentiful.

Makes 4 servings

4 (6½-inch) pita bread rounds

2 tomatoes, thinly sliced

2 garlic cloves, thinly sliced

4 large scallions, chopped

¼ pound feta cheese, crumbled

8 kalamata olives, pitted and chopped

½ teaspoon dried oregano

1 Preheat the oven to 425°F.

2 Place the pita rounds on a baking sheet in a single layer. Arrange the tomato slices on the rounds in an overlapping circular pattern. Sprinkle with the garlic, scallions, feta cheese, olives, and oregano. Bake until the cheese softens and the bread crisps, about 8 minutes.

What's for Lunch

Serve with a cucumber and red onion salad dressed with balsamic vinaigrette.

 COOK'S TIP Vary the pizza according to your whim by using one of the many different varieties of flavored feta cheese available in your supermarket.

Per serving:
268 Calories • 8 g Total Fat • 4 g Saturated Fat • 25 mg Cholesterol • 709 mg Sodium • 40 mg Total Carbohydrate
3 g Dietary Fiber • 10 g Protein • 216 mg Calcium

5 *POINTS* per serving

Penne with Cherry Tomatoes, Provolone, and Broccoli

The colors of the Italian flag are mirrored by the red tomatoes, cream-colored cheese, and green broccoli all teamed with penne in this abundant Italian-style dish. A small amount of intensely flavored sharp provolone adds great flavor without a lot of unwanted fat.

Makes 4 servings (yield 7 cups)

1/2 pound penne

2 1/2 cups broccoli florets

1 tablespoon olive oil

3 garlic cloves, thinly sliced

1 pint cherry tomatoes

1/2 teaspoon salt

1/4 teaspoon coarsely ground black pepper

2 ounces sharp provolone cheese, shredded

2 tablespoons grated Parmesan cheese

1 Bring a large pot of salted water to a boil. Add the pasta and cook according to package directions, adding the broccoli to the pot during the last 2 minutes of cooking. Drain.

2 Heat the oil in a large nonstick skillet over medium-high heat. Add the garlic and cook, stirring occasionally, until lightly golden, about 1 minute. Add the tomatoes and cook until the skins begin to blister slightly, about 1 minute. Add the pasta and broccoli, salt, and pepper; cook 2 minutes longer to heat through. Transfer to a large bowl; stir in the cheeses.

What's for Lunch

 Serve this hearty meal with mineral water spiked with rosé wine and fresh lime wedges.

COOK'S TIP Since provolone becomes much more robustly flavored as it ages, select an aged provolone for this dish.

7 POINTS **per serving**

Per serving:
338 Calories • 9 g Total Fat • 4 g Saturated Fat • 12 mg Cholesterol • 559 mg Sodium • 50 mg Total Carbohydrate 4 g Dietary Fiber • 14 g Protein • 185 mg Calcium

Grilled Vegetable Sandwiches

There's nothing quite like the taste of food that's been grilled outdoors. When grilling, cutting vegetables to just the right thickness—about 1/4-inch—is important. If the vegetables are sliced too thin, they may burn. If too thick, they won't be flavorful.

Makes 4 servings

1 (3/4-pound) eggplant, cut into 1/4-inch slices

1 medium zucchini, cut on the diagonal into 1/4-inch slices

1 medium yellow squash, cut on the diagonal into 1/4-inch slices

3/4 teaspoon salt

3/4 teaspoon coarsely ground black pepper

1/4 cup reduced-calorie mayonnaise

1 teaspoon fresh rosemary, chopped

8 slices Italian bread, toasted

1 cup loosely packed arugula

2 tomatoes, thinly sliced

1/2 small red onion, thinly sliced

1/4 cup shredded Parmesan cheese

1 Preheat the grill or broiler. Spray the eggplant, zucchini, and yellow squash lightly with nonstick spray; sprinkle with the salt and pepper. Grill or broil (4 inches from the heat, on a baking sheet or the rack of a broiler pan) until tender and browned, about 8 minutes, turning so that the vegetables are browned all over.

2 Meanwhile, combine the mayonnaise and rosemary in a small bowl; spread on 4 slices of the toast. Layer the grilled vegetables over the spread. Top with equal amounts of the arugula, tomatoes, and onion. Sprinkle with the Parmesan cheese and cover with the remaining toast; cut each sandwich in half on the diagonal.

What's for Lunch

Pair this healthy midday meal with a comforting cup of chicken noodle soup.

 COOK'S TIP Nonstick spray now comes in several varieties; olive oil nonstick spray works particularly well in this recipe.

5 POINTS per serving

Per serving:
272 Calories • 7 g Total Fat • 2 g Saturated Fat • 9 mg Cholesterol • 1,022 mg Sodium • 44 mg Total Carbohydrate
6 g Dietary Fiber • 10 g Protein • 156 mg Calcium

Curried Eggless Salad Sandwich

*Makes 6 servings
(yield 2 cups)*

1 (1-pound) package
soft tofu, drained

6 tablespoons reduced-
calorie mayonnaise

1 tablespoon curry powder

1/4 teaspoon salt

1/4 teaspoon coarsely
ground black pepper

6 whole-wheat rolls,
split open

2 tomatoes, sliced

3 cups alfalfa sprouts

If you've been depriving yourself of egg salad because of the cholesterol and calories in egg yolks, this recipe is for you! We make it with cholesterol-free tofu (instead of eggs) which tends to take on the flavors of other, more assertive ingredients. Here, it is teamed up with pungent curry powder, making for a slightly spicy salad. For extra crunch, add diced celery and shredded carrot.

 1 Mash the tofu with a fork in a bowl. Stir in the mayonnaise, curry powder, salt, and pepper.

2 Spoon the mixture onto the bottom halves of the rolls. Top with the tomato slices and alfalfa sprouts; cover with the roll tops.

What's for Lunch

This sandwich goes well with a chilled summer soup, such as gazpacho or vichyssoise.

 COOK'S TIP This flavorful filling could also be used to stuff tomatoes for a light lunch.

4 POINTS per serving

Per serving:
204 Calories • 8g Total Fat • 31g Saturated Fat • 15 mg Cholesterol • 410 mg Sodium • 25 mg Total Carbohydrate
3g Dietary Fiber • 10 g Protein • 119 mg Calcium

Creamy Cauliflower Soup

Fat-free half-and-half gives this soup its rich creaminess, the leeks add a savory accent and the nutmeg lends a final pinch of sweetness.

*Makes 6 servings
(yield 8¹/₂ cups)*

1 tablespoon olive oil

2 leeks, cleaned and chopped (about 1¹/₂ cups)

6 cups reduced-sodium chicken broth

2 (1-pound) bags frozen cauliflower, thawed

¹/₂ cup fat-free half-and-half

¹/₈ teaspoon ground nutmeg

1 Heat the oil in a large nonstick saucepan over medium heat. Add the leeks and cook, stirring frequently, until softened but not browned, about 4 minutes. Add the broth and cauliflower; bring to a boil. Cover and simmer until the cauliflower is tender, about 10 minutes. Remove from the heat and stir in the half-and-half and nutmeg.

2 Puree the soup with a hand-held immersible blender, or in a food processor, or blender, in batches if necessary.

What's for Lunch

Pair this rich soup with watercress or smoked salmon tea sandwiches spread with reduced-fat mayonnaise.

 COOK'S TIP A hand-held immersion blender comes in handy in this recipe since it allows you to puree the soup right in the pot, rather than having to transfer it to a food processor or blender.

1 *POINT* per serving

Per serving (generous 1¹/₃ cup):
100 Calories • 2 g Total Fat • 0 g Saturated Fat • 0 mg Cholesterol • 623 mg Sodium • 11 mg Total Carbohydrate
4 g Dietary Fiber • 7 g Protein • 46 mg Calcium

Corn-Tortilla Soup

Instead of adding flour or cornstarch, this soup is thickened with corn tortillas, which add flavor as well as body. Any stewed tomatoes will do; one of the seasoned varieties, such as Mexican-style, will provide added zest to the soup.

Makes 4 servings
(yield about 7 cups)

1 tablespoon olive oil

1 onion, chopped

1 green bell pepper, seeded and chopped

1 garlic clove, chopped

2 (6-inch) corn tortillas, coarsely chopped

4 cups reduced-sodium chicken broth

1 (14½-ounce) can stewed tomatoes, with their juice

1 (10-ounce) box frozen corn kernels

1 medium-large all-purpose potato, peeled and cubed

¼ cup chopped cilantro

Heat the oil in a large saucepan. Sauté the onion, bell pepper, and garlic until the onion is tender, about 5 minutes. Add the tortillas, broth, tomatoes, corn, and potato; bring to a boil. Cover, reduce the heat, and simmer until the vegetables are tender, about 10 minutes. Stir in the cilantro.

What's for Lunch

A basket of baked corn chips and a dark green salad turn this lunch into something memorable.

COOK'S TIP For a more substantial soup, stir ¾ pound skinless boneless chicken breasts, cut into thin strips, into the soup to cook with the vegetables.

4 *POINTS* per serving

Per serving (1¾ cups):
228 Calories • 5 g Total Fat • 1 g Saturated Fat • 0 mg Cholesterol • 817 mg Sodium • 43 mg Total Carbohydrate 5 g Dietary Fiber • 9 g Protein • 93 mg Calcium

Vegetable Garden Soup with Basil

Makes 8 servings
(yield 11 cups)

2 medium red potatoes, cubed

1 onion, chopped

1 carrot, chopped

6 cups reduced-sodium chicken broth

1 medium zucchini, diced

1 medium yellow squash, diced

2 cups frozen cut green beans

1 cup frozen peas

1 cup chopped fresh basil

1/4 cup grated Parmesan cheese

Think of this dish as a soup for all seasons: In the summer when squash and fresh basil are abundant, it makes good use of your garden's crop. Later in the year, you can substitute a thawed ten-ounce box of frozen chopped spinach for the basil.

Combine the potatoes, onion, carrot, and broth in a large saucepan. Bring to a boil. Cover, reduce the heat, and simmer until the potatoes are just tender, about 10 minutes. Add the zucchini, yellow squash, beans, and peas. Continue cooking until the vegetables are tender, about 10 minutes longer. Remove from the heat and stir in the basil and cheese.

What's for Lunch

All you need to round out the meal is toasted pita bread and hummus.

COOK'S TIP   Whether you make it with basil or spinach, this soup freezes well. To reheat, thaw the soup overnight in the refrigerator, then heat it thoroughly by bringing to a boil.

1 *POINT* per serving

Per serving:
100 Calories • 1 g Total Fat • 1 g Saturated Fat • 2 mg Cholesterol • 490 mg Sodium • 17 mg Total Carbohydrate
4 g Dietary Fiber • 7 g Protein • 88 mg Calcium

LUNCH

Coconut Fruit Cocktail

This contemporary update of classic ambrosia salad makes a perfect addition to a summer buffet. You can substitute fresh pineapple for canned (look for it peeled and prepped in the produce section of your market). For a pretty presentation, spoon the fruit into cracked coconut shells before serving and garnish with sprigs of mint.

Makes 8 servings
(yield 8 cups)

1/4 cup light pancake syrup

3 tablespoons orange juice

1 tablespoon grated orange zest

1/2 teaspoon ground ginger

1 (20-ounce) can pineapple chunks in juice, drained

1 (15-ounce) can Mandarin oranges in light syrup, drained

2 small bananas, cut into 1/4-inch rounds

2 small peaches, sliced

1 1/2 cups fresh raspberries

1 cup fresh blueberries

1/2 cup flaked coconut, toasted

Whisk together the syrup, orange juice, orange zest, and ginger in a small bowl. Combine the pineapple, oranges, bananas, peaches, raspberries, and blueberries in a large bowl. Stir in the syrup mixture and sprinkle with the coconut.

What's for Lunch

 Serve with low-fat cottage cheese for a light lunch.

COOK'S TIP To toast coconut, spread it evenly on a baking sheet. Toast, stirring frequently, in a preheated 350°F oven until lightly browned, seven to ten minutes. You can also toast it in a microwave oven on High, stirring several times, for five minutes.

3 *POINTS* per serving

Per serving:
162 Calories • 2 g Total Fat • 1 g Saturated Fat • 0 mg Cholesterol • 21 mg Sodium • 38 mg Total Carbohydrate • 4 g Dietary Fiber • 1 g Protein • 25 mg Calcium

Catfish and Coleslaw Po' Boys

Po' Boys are New Orleans' distinctive and spicy submarine sandwiches, usually made on French or Italian bread. They were named after "poor boys," or local workers who, during the city's lean times, would knock on the back doors of New Orleans' restaurants looking for handouts. Restaurateurs would give them bits of leftovers in crusty bread loaves—thus, the name of this Louisiana classic.

Makes 4 servings

1/2 cup plain dried bread crumbs

1 1/2 teaspoons paprika

1 teaspoon garlic powder

1/2 teaspoon dried thyme

1/4 teaspoon cayenne

3/4 teaspoon salt

1 large egg white

2 tablespoons fat-free milk

4 (6-ounce) catfish fillets

3 cups shredded cabbage salad (coleslaw mix)

3 tablespoons cider vinegar

2 tablespoons sugar

1 tablespoon Creole mustard or course-grained Dijon mustard

8 ounces Italian bread (about 1/2 loaf), split open and cut crosswise into 4 sandwiches

1 Preheat the oven to 450°F. Coat the rack of a baking sheet with nonstick spray.

2 Combine the bread crumbs, paprika, garlic powder, thyme, cayenne, and 1/4 teaspoon of the salt on a plate. In a bowl, combine the egg white and milk. Dip each fillet into the milk mixture to moisten, and then into the bread crumb mixture to coat; place on the baking sheet. Spray lightly with nonstick spray and bake until just opaque in the center, 10–12 minutes.

3 Meanwhile, combine the cabbage, vinegar, sugar, mustard, and the remaining 1/2 teaspoon salt in a bowl. Layer each sandwich bottom with a catfish fillet and an equal amount of the coleslaw. Top with the sandwich tops.

What's for Lunch

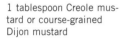 Perfect paired with oven baked "fried" potatoes. To make: toss thin potato slices in a bit of oil, and bake in a preheated 300°F oven until browned, 15–20 minutes, turning the chips after ten minutes.

 For authentic Big Easy spiciness, spike the sandwiches with hot sauce.

10 *POINTS* per serving

Per serving:
464 Calories • 14 g Total Fat • 3 g Saturated Fat • 82 mg Cholesterol • 1,044 mg Sodium • 51 mg Total Carbohydrate
4 g Dietary Fiber • 33 g Protein • 138 mg Calcium

Minted Buttermilk Pea Soup with Crab

This creamy seafood soup is delightful served at room temperature. Or, for a change of pace, make it ahead of time, cover, and chill it in the refrigerator. The soup is also very good made with steamed shrimp instead of crabmeat.

Makes 4 servings
(yield 4 cups)

1 tablespoon butter

2 onions, chopped

1 3/4 cups fat-free, reduced-sodium chicken broth

1 (10-ounce) package frozen peas

1 cup low-fat buttermilk

2 tablespoons chopped fresh mint

1/4 teaspoon salt

1/8 teaspoon coarsely ground black pepper

1/2 pound cooked lump crabmeat, picked over to remove any shell

Melt the butter in a large saucepan over medium-high heat. Add the onions and cook, stirring often, until softened, about 4 minutes. Stir in the broth and peas and bring to a boil. Reduce the heat and simmer 5 minutes. Remove the soup from the heat and stir in the buttermilk, mint, salt, and pepper. Puree the soup in a blender or food processor, in batches if necessary. Divide the soup into 4 bowls and sprinkle the crab on top.

What's for Lunch

Serve the soup with a watercress salad, some crusty bread, and a chilled glass of a crisp, white wine.

COOK'S TIP Be sure to remove the saucepan from the heat before adding the buttermilk, otherwise it will curdle.

4 POINTS per serving

Per serving (1 cup):
197 Calories • 5 g Total Fat • 2 g Saturated Fat • 67 mg Cholesterol • 728 mg Sodium • 18 mg Total Carbohydrate • 4 g Dietary Fiber • 20 g Protein • 157 mg Calcium

Shrimp and Corn Chowder

Thick, rich, and often seafood-based, chowders have been a part of the American culinary heritage for generations. When succulent fresh corn is in season, you may want to substitute four cups of kernels fresh off the cob; for the frozen corn. Either way you'll enjoy the warming effects of this flavorful concoction.

*Makes 6 servings
(yield 7 cups)*

1 tablespoon butter

2 (10-ounce) packages frozen corn, thawed

1 onion, chopped

2 (8-ounce) bottles clam juice

1³/4 cups fat-free, reduced-sodium chicken broth

2 teaspoons sugar

¹/2 teaspoon cayenne

¹/2 teaspoon dried thyme

³/4 pound medium shrimp, peeled and deveined

¹/2 teaspoon salt

Melt the butter in a large saucepan over medium–high heat. Add the corn and onion and cook, stirring occasionally, until softened, 8–10 minutes. Add the clam juice, broth, sugar, cayenne, and thyme; bring to a boil. Reduce the heat and simmer 5 minutes. Transfer to a blender and puree, in batches if necessary. Return to the saucepan over medium–high heat and bring to a simmer. Stir in the shrimp and salt and cook until the shrimp are pink, about 2 minutes.

What's for Lunch

 Serve the chowder with crispy bagel chips

COOK'S TIP To strip fresh corn off the cob, stand the ear upright on a chopping board and slice down with a sharp knife to release the kernels. Or, use a serrated corn stripper, available from kitchenware stores.

Per serving (1 generous cup):
173 Calories • 4 g Total Fat • 1 g Saturated Fat • 80 mg Cholesterol • 629 mg Sodium • 24 mg Total Carbohydrate
1 g Dietary Fiber • 14 g Protein • 48 mg Calcium

4 POINTS per serving

Sea Scallop Salad

Light, citrus accented, and dotted with olives, oranges, and onion, this seafood salad has a distinctly Mediterranean feel, particularly if you add the optional mint.

Makes 4 servings

1 pound sea scallops

1/2 teaspoon coarsely ground black pepper

3/4 teaspoon salt

1/4 cup orange juice

2 tablespoons olive oil

1 tablespoon fresh lemon juice

1 teaspoon honey

2 navel oranges, peeled and coarsely chopped

1 ruby red grapefruit, peeled and coarsely chopped

1/2 cup thinly sliced red onion

6 oil-cured black olives, pitted

4 cups mesclun

2 tablespoons chopped fresh mint (optional)

1 Heat a large nonstick skillet over medium-high heat; spray with non-stick spray. Sprinkle the scallops with the pepper and 1/2 teaspoon of the salt. Sauté the scallops until browned on the outside and opaque in the center, 3–4 minutes.

2 Meanwhile, whisk together the orange juice, oil, lemon juice, honey, and the remaining 1/4 teaspoon salt in a large bowl. Add the oranges, grapefruit, onion, and olives. Stir in the scallops.

3 Divide the mesclun among 4 plates; top each with an equal amount of the scallop salad. Garnish with mint if desired.

What's for Lunch

 A glass of Chianti and some crusty Italian bread—what more could you ask for?

 COOK'S TIP Thoroughly pat the scallops dry with paper towels before you sauté them, and arrange in a single layer in the skillet, making sure they don't touch each other; otherwise they will steam instead of brown.

5 POINTS per serving

Per serving:
251 Calories • 9 g Total Fat • 1 g Saturated Fat • 37 mg Cholesterol • 677 mg Sodium • 23 mg Total Carbohydrate • 4 g Dietary Fiber • 21 g Protein • 99 mg Calcium

Sea Scallop Salad

LUNCH

Spring Shrimp Salad

Make this salad in the spring and early summer, when fresh asparagus is plentiful.
If yellow tomatoes are available, use them for a festive presentation.

Makes 4 servings

1 bunch asparagus, trimmed and cut into 2-inch pieces

1 pound peeled cooked medium shrimp

2 tomatoes, quartered

2 large scallions, chopped

2 tablespoons chopped cilantro

2 tablespoons fresh lime juice

1 1/2 tablespoons extra-virgin olive oil

2 teaspoons honey

1/4 teaspoon salt

1/4 teaspoon coarsely ground black pepper

 Cook the asparagus in a large pot of boiling water until crisp-tender, about 5 minutes; drain and rinse under cool running water. Transfer to a large bowl. Add the shrimp, tomatoes, scallions, and cilantro.

 Whisk together the lime juice, oil, honey, salt, and pepper in a small bowl. Toss with the asparagus mixture.

What's for Lunch

Serve the shrimp salad at room temperature over chilled soba noodles.

COOK'S TIP Serve the salad at once while still warm, or cover and refrigerate. A tablespoon or two of tequila stirred into the lime juice mixture adds a tasty kick.

4 POINTS per serving

Per serving:
203 Calories • 7 g Total Fat • 1 g Saturated Fat • 221 mg Cholesterol • 417 mg Sodium • 8 mg Total Carbohydrate
2 g Dietary Fiber • 26 g Protein • 64 mg Calcium

Chunky Gazpacho Salad with Shrimp

This satisfying main dish salad includes many of the ingredients used in a classic gazpacho, but let your blender sit this one out. The long thin seedless cucumber works best here. It may be called a gourmet or an English cucumber in the supermarket.

Makes 4 servings

3/4 cup spicy vegetable juice

2 tablespoons red wine vinegar

1 tablespoon olive oil

1 tablespoon Worcestershire sauce

1/4 teaspoon salt

1/4 teaspoon coarsely ground black pepper

1 pound peeled cooked small shrimp

1 medium seedless cucumber, peeled and cut into 3/4-inch chunks (about 2 cups)

1 pint cherry or grape tomatoes, halved

1 green bell pepper, seeded and chopped

4 large scallions, chopped

1/2 cup chopped cilantro

1/4 cup thinly sliced red onion

4 green or red lettuce leaves

 Whisk together the vegetable juice, vinegar, oil, Worcestershire sauce, salt, and black pepper in a large bowl. Stir in the shrimp, cucumber, tomatoes, bell pepper, scallions, cilantro, and onion; toss to coat.

2 Line a platter with the lettuce leaves. Spoon the shrimp mixture on top.

What's for Lunch

Try serving this shrimp and vegetable salad with crisp crackers, such as rusks. Or, sprinkle a few garlic croutons over the salad before serving.

4 POINTS per serving

Per serving:
202 Calories • 5 g Total Fat • 1 g Saturated Fat • 221 mg Cholesterol • 605 mg Sodium • 13 mg Total Carbohydrate 3 g Dietary Fiber • 26 g Protein • 94 mg Calcium

Confetti Shrimp Salad with Lemon Mayonnaise

Dotted with bits of bell pepper, onion, and dill, this refreshing salad is as bright and colorful as a summer afternoon. You can also serve the salad as a sandwich; just tuck it into pitas or pile it on toasted slices of sourdough bread.

Makes 4 servings (yield 3 cups)

¹/₄ cup reduced-calorie mayonnaise

1 teaspoon coarse-grained Dijon mustard

2 teaspoons grated lemon zest

2 teaspoons fresh lemon juice

¹/₈ teaspoon salt

1 pound peeled cooked medium shrimp

¹/₂ cup seeded and chopped yellow bell pepper

¹/₂ cup seeded and chopped red bell pepper

4 large scallions, chopped

¹/₄ cup chopped red onion

2 tablespoons chopped fresh dill

Whisk together the mayonnaise, mustard, lemon zest, lemon juice, and salt in a large bowl. Add the shrimp, bell peppers, scallions, onion, and dill; toss to coat. If not serving immediately, cover and refrigerate until ready to serve.

What's for Lunch

For Middle Eastern flair, serve the dish with Tabbouleh salad and lavasch flatbread, found in the cracker section of your supermarket.

 COOK'S TIP If you really feel like splurging, substitute lobster or crabmeat for the shrimp.

3 POINTS per serving

Per serving:
159 Calories • 3 g Total Fat • 0 g Saturated Fat • 226 mg Cholesterol • 467 mg Sodium • 6 mg Total Carbohydrate
1 g Dietary Fiber • 25 g Protein • 65 mg Calcium

Cool Shrimp and Mango Salad

Try this tropical treat on a sweltering summer day. When buying mangoes, look for a yellowish outer skin tinged with red, which is a sign of ripeness. If you can't find ripe mangoes, papayas will work just as well.

Makes 4 servings

3 tablespoons orange juice

2 tablespoons fresh lime juice

1 tablespoon honey

1 teaspoon Dijon mustard

1 teaspoon olive oil

$1/4$ teaspoon salt

Pinch of crushed red pepper

1 pound peeled cooked medium or large shrimp

2 ripe mangoes, peeled and cut into $3/4$-inch chunks

$1/4$ cup chopped fresh mint

4 cups baby spinach, cleaned

Whisk together the orange juice, lime juice, honey, mustard, oil, salt, and crushed red pepper in a large bowl. Stir in the shrimp, mangoes, and mint. Arrange the spinach on a platter and top with the salad.

What's for Lunch

Garnish the salad with rice crackers and serve with tall glasses of iced tea.

4 POINTS per serving

Per serving:
223 Calories • 3 g Total Fat • 1 g Saturated Fat • 221 mg Cholesterol • 434 mg Sodium • 25 mg Total Carbohydrate
3 g Dietary Fiber • 25 g Protein • 100 mg Calcium

Asian Glazed Tuna Steak Sandwiches

The tuna marinade in this recipe works equally well with chicken breasts, pork tenderloin, scallops, or salmon steaks. It's also an easy make-ahead marinade that can be stored in the refrigerator for a day or two after preparation.

Makes 4 servings

4 tablespoons reduced-sodium soy sauce

5 teaspoons Asian (dark) sesame oil

2 tablespoons rice vinegar

1 tablespoon honey

4 (6-ounce) tuna steaks

6 tablespoons reduced-fat mayonnaise

2 large scallions, chopped

1 teaspoon hot pepper sauce

4 lettuce leaves (optional)

8 (1-ounce) slices sourdough bread, toasted

1. Combine 3 tablespoons of the soy sauce, 2 teaspoons of the oil, the vinegar, and honey in a bowl. Add the tuna, turning to coat, and let stand 5 minutes. Meanwhile, combine the mayonnaise, scallions, the remaining 1 tablespoon soy sauce, 1 teaspoon of the oil, and the pepper sauce in a second bowl.

2. Heat the remaining 2 teaspoons oil in a large nonstick skillet over medium-high heat. Add the tuna and cook until pink in the middle, 3–4 minutes on each side.

3. Place a lettuce leaf on each of 4 slices of toast, if desired. Top with a tuna steak on each; spread with the mayonnaise mixture, and cover with the remaining slices of toast.

What's for Lunch

The tuna sandwich is complemented nicely by thinly sliced beefsteak tomatoes.

10 *POINTS* per serving

Per serving:
476 Calories • 14 g Total Fat • 3 g Saturated Fat • 81 mg Cholesterol • 918 mg Sodium • 39 mg Total Carbohydrate • 2 g Dietary Fiber • 45 g Protein • 80 mg Calcium

Chicken Barley Soup

Barley is an ancient grain that has been used for centuries to make soups, breads, porridges, and, when malted, beer and whiskey. Traditionally known as a long cooking grain, this satisfying soup can be made in minutes, thanks to the quick-cooking varieties now available. Do not use reduced-sodium broth in this recipe—you'll want the salt to season the soup.

Makes 4 servings

1 pound skinless boneless chicken breasts, cubed

1/2 teaspoon salt

1/4 teaspoon coarsely ground black pepper

1 teaspoon canola oil

1 3/4 cups chicken broth

5 cups water

1/2 cup quick-cooking barley

1 (10-ounce) package Italian-style frozen vegetables

Sprinkle the chicken with the salt and pepper. Heat the oil in a large non-stick saucepan. Add the chicken and cook until browned, about 5 minutes. Add the broth and water; bring to a boil. Add the barley, cover, reduce the heat, and simmer until the barley is tender, about 10 minutes. Stir in the vegetables and cook until tender, about 5 minutes longer.

What's for Lunch

Finish the meal with a medley of mixed sliced melon and tiny cookies.

4 POINTS per serving

Per serving:
231 Calories • 4 g Total Fat • 1 g Saturated Fat • 66 mg Cholesterol • 823 mg Sodium • 18 mg Total Carbohydrate 3 g Dietary Fiber • 30 g Protein • 34 mg Calcium

Chicken Cheddar Hoagies

Reminiscent of Philadelphia's famed cheese steak sandwiches, these hoagies are a snap to make and have only a fraction of the fat of the original version.

Makes 4 servings

2 teaspoons olive oil

1 large onion, thinly sliced

1 red bell pepper, seeded and thinly sliced

1 green bell pepper, seeded and thinly sliced

1/2 teaspoon dried thyme

1 tablespoon Worcestershire sauce

1/2 teaspoon salt

1/4 teaspoon coarsely ground black pepper

4 (4-ounce) thin-sliced skinless boneless chicken breasts

1/2 cup shredded reduced-fat sharp cheddar cheese

8 ounces Italian bread (about 1/2 loaf), split part open and cut crosswise into 4 sandwiches.

1 Heat 1 teaspoon of the oil in a large nonstick skillet over medium-high heat. Add the onion, bell peppers, and thyme; cook, stirring occasionally, until softened, 4–5 minutes. Add the Worcestershire sauce, 1/4 teaspoon of the salt, and 1/8 teaspoon of the black pepper; cook 2 minutes. Transfer to a bowl.

2 Sprinkle the chicken with the remaining 1/4 teaspoon salt and 1/8 teaspoon black pepper. Heat the remaining 1 teaspoon oil in the skillet. Add the chicken and cook 3 minutes. Turn the chicken over and top each piece with 1/4 cup of the onion mixture and 2 tablespoons of the cheese. Cover the pan and cook until the cheese melts, about 2 minutes.

3 Meanwhile, mound 1/4 cup of the remaining onion mixture onto each of the sandwich bottoms; top with the chicken and cover with the tops.

What's for Lunch

A salad of baby lettuce adds a light touch and rounds out this hearty meal.

8 POINTS per serving

Per serving:
387 Calories • 9 g Total Fat • 3 g Saturated Fat • 80 mg Cholesterol • 814 mg Sodium • 38 mg Total Carbohydrate 4 g Dietary Fiber • 37 g Protein • 205 mg Calcium

Chicken, Basil, and Roasted Pepper Panini

Makes 4 servings

6 teaspoons olive oil

4 (4-ounce) skinless bone-less chicken breasts

2 tablespoons balsamic vinegar

1 tablespoon Dijon mustard

$1/4$ teaspoon salt

$1/8$ teaspoon coarsely ground black pepper

2 (4-ounce) Italian rolls, (such as ciabatta) split open

$1/4$ cup basil leaves

2 jarred roasted sweet red peppers, drained and halved

The word panini, *Italian for rolls or small breads, is usually used to describe the small grilled sandwiches that are so popular throughout Italy. The flavor combinations are practically limitless so use your imagination to create your favorite variations. For example, for a no-cook meal, thin slices of roast beef or cooked fresh tuna will work nicely in place of the chicken. Or, try a version that teams chopped spinach with thin slices of fresh mozzarella.*

 Heat 2 teaspoons of the oil in a large nonstick skillet over medium-high heat. Add the chicken and cook until lightly browned and cooked through, about 5 minutes on each side.

2 Meanwhile, combine the vinegar, mustard, salt, and pepper in a bowl. Slowly whisk in the remaining 4 teaspoons oil. Brush the inside of each roll with the mixture. Divide the basil, roasted peppers, and chicken between the bottom halves of the rolls. Cover with the tops and cut each sandwich in half crosswise.

What's for Lunch

Serve the panini with oven-baked sweet potato chips.

 Make your own sweet potato chips by tossing thin sweet potato slices in oil. Bake them in a preheated 300°F oven, turning the chips after ten minutes, until browned, 15–20 minutes.

8 *POINTS* per serving

Per serving:
371 Calories • 12 g Total Fat • 2 g Saturated Fat • 72 mg Cholesterol • 621 mg Sodium • 31 mg Total Carbohydrate 2 g Dietary Fiber • 32 g Protein • 69 mg Calcium

LUNCH

California Chicken Salad

This dish is reminiscent of a Cobb salad, with its ingredients arranged in neat rows on a platter to be tossed just before eating. To serve with a flourish, toss tableside.

*Makes 4 servings
(yield about 6 cups)*

1¾ cups fat-free, reduced-sodium chicken broth

1 pound skinless boneless chicken breasts

1 cup seedless green grapes, halved

1 tomato, cut into thin wedges

1 Granny Smith apple, cored and cut into thin slices

1 orange, peeled and cut into segments

1 scant cup thinly sliced avocado (preferably Hass)

⅓ cup thinly sliced red onion

¼ cup orange juice

2 teaspoons Dijon mustard

½ teaspoon salt

⅛ teaspoon coarsely ground black pepper

 Bring the broth to a boil in a skillet over medium-high heat. Add the chicken, reduce the heat, and simmer until cooked through, about 10 minutes. Remove the chicken from the broth and allow to cool 2 minutes. Cut the chicken against the grain into thin slices and arrange in a row across the center of a platter. (Reserve the broth for future use in soups, sauces, etc.)

 Arrange the grapes, tomato, apple, orange, avocado, and onion in rows alongside the chicken. Combine the orange juice, mustard, salt, and pepper in a small bowl. Drizzle the dressing over the salad.

What's for Lunch

Serve the salad with an all-American bread, such as Parkerhouse rolls or popovers.

 COOK'S TIP To help prevent food-borne illness, don't leave leftovers out for more than two hours. If the dish contains meat, fish, poultry, or dairy foods, place it in the refrigerator within one hour after cooking.

5 POINTS per serving

Per serving:
263 Calories • 7 g Total Fat • 2 g Saturated Fat • 72 mg Cholesterol • 409 mg Sodium • 22 mg Total Carbohydrate
4 g Dietary Fiber • 28 g Protein • 45 mg Calcium

Buffalo Chicken Bites

This easy-to-make dish—perfect for a buffet—has all the flavor of Buffalo chicken wings without all the added calories and fat For extra heat, add more hot pepper sauce and a pinch or two of cayenne.

Makes 4 servings

1/4 cup Louisiana-style hot sauce

1 teaspoon hot pepper sauce (Tabasco)

1 teaspoon Worcestershire sauce

2 tablespoons butter

1 pound skinless boneless chicken breasts, cut into 1-inch chunks

2 carrots, cut into sticks

3 celery stalks, cut into sticks

1/2 cup fat-free bluc cheese dressing

 Combine the hot sauce, pepper sauce, and Worcestershire sauce in a small saucepan over medium heat; bring to a boil and cook 1 minute. Remove from the heat and add 5 teaspoons of the butter, stirring until melted.

2 Melt the remaining 1 teaspoon of the butter in a large nonstick skillet over medium-high heat. Add the chicken and cook, stirring frequently, until well browned, 8–10 minutes. Add the pepper sauce mixture and cook for about 1 minute longer, tossing the chicken to coat. Serve with the carrots, celery, and blue cheese dressing.

What's for Lunch

Pair with crusty hard rolls

 COOK'S TIP Prep twice as much of the carrots and celery stalks called for so that you'll have extra for a healthy snack another time.

---

5 POINTS per serving

Per serving:
246 Calories • 8 g Total Fat • 4 g Saturated Fat • 82 mg Cholesterol • 1,340 mg Sodium • 16 mg Total Carbohydrate
2 g Dietary Fiber • 27 g Protein • 36 mg Calcium

Turkey Club Salad with Creamy Peppercorn Dressing

Just like a bacon, lettuce, and tomato sandwich, only in salad form; this dish is also a tasty way to use leftover turkey.

*Makes 4 servings
(yield 8 cups salad;
³/4 cup dressing)*

6 slices turkey bacon, diced

¹/2 cup reduced-calorie mayonnaise

¹/4 cup fat-free half-and-half

1 tablespoon fresh lemon juice

1 teaspoon Dijon mustard

³/4 teaspoon coarsely ground black pepper

8 cups mixed salad greens

2 cups cubed cooked turkey breast

10 cherry tomatoes, halved

1 cup plain croutons

 Spray a nonstick skillet with nonstick spray. Cook the bacon until browned, about 3 minutes.

 Whisk together the mayonnaise, half-and-half, lemon juice, mustard, and pepper in a large bowl. Add the greens, turkey, tomatoes, and croutons. Sprinkle with the bacon; toss to coat.

What's for Lunch

Start the meal with a cup of low-fat cream of celery or broccoli soup.

COOK'S TIP If you don't have any leftover turkey on hand, use ¹/2 pound deli-sliced turkey, chopped.

6 *POINTS* per serving

Per serving:
274 Calories • 11 g Total Fat • 2 g Saturated Fat • 74 mg Cholesterol • 683 mg Sodium • 14 mg Total Carbohydrate
2 g Dietary Fiber • 27 g Protein • 77 mg Calcium

Antipasto Salad

Luscious cheese-filled tortellini are the main attraction in this hearty main-course salad, brimming with the ingredients you would expect to find on an antipasto plate at your favorite Italian trattoria.

*Makes 6 servings
(yield 8 cups)*

1 (9-ounce) package frozen low-fat cheese tortellini

2 celery stalks, chopped

1 cup cherry tomatoes, halved

1/2 cup sliced pitted black olives

1/2 cup thinly sliced red onion

1/2 cup chopped fresh basil

2 (1-ounce) slices reduced-fat turkey salami, cut into 1/4-inch strips

2 (1-ounce) slices fat-free turkey breast, cut into 1/4-inch strips

2 (1-ounce) slices fat-free turkey ham, cut into 1/4-inch strips

2 (1-ounce) slices provolone cheese, cut into 1/4-inch strips

3 tablespoons red wine vinegar

1 tablespoon extra-virgin olive oil

 1 Prepare the tortellini according to package directions. Rinse under cool running water; drain.

2 Combine the celery, tomatoes, olives, onion, basil, salami, turkey breast, turkey ham, and cheese in a large bowl. Add the tortellini, vinegar, and oil. Toss to coat. Serve at once while still warm, or cover and refrigerate.

What's for Lunch

Serve this colorful salad on a bed of romaine lettuce or mesclun.

 COOK'S TIP Be sure to rinse the cooked tortellini under cool running water to prevent it from sticking when you add it to the other ingredients.

5 *POINTS* per serving

Per serving (1 1/3 cups):
220 Calories • 9 g Total Fat • 3 g Saturated Fat • 43 mg Cholesterol • 676 mg Sodium • 25 mg Total Carbohydrate • 2 g Dietary Fiber • 14 g Protein • 127 mg Calcium

L U N C H

Turkey Fattoush

Fattoush *is the Middle Eastern version of a popular Italian bread salad, panzanella. We've substituted toasted pita for the crusty Italian bread and added turkey, making it a hearty one-dish meal.*

Makes 4 servings
(yield 8 cups)

2 tablespoons + 2 tea-spoons extra-virgin olive oil

1 pound turkey breast cut-lets, cut into thin strips

$^1/_2$ teaspoon salt

$^1/_4$ teaspoon coarsely ground black pepper

3 (6$^1/_2$-inch) pita bread rounds

2 tomatoes, seeded and chopped

1 cucumber, peeled, halved lengthwise, seeded, and sliced

$^1/_2$ cup thinly sliced red onion

3 tablespoons balsamic vinegar

3 tablespoons thinly sliced fresh mint

$^3/_4$ teaspoon ground cumin

1 Heat 2 teaspoons of the oil in a large nonstick skillet over med-ium-high heat. Sprinkle the turkey with $^1/_4$ teaspoon of the salt and $^1/_8$ teaspoon of the pepper. Cook, stirring occasionally, until the turkey is lightly browned and cooked through, 5–6 minutes; transfer to a large bowl.

2 Toast the pita rounds and cut them in half (do not split open). Cut each half into scant $^1/_4$-inch strips; add to the bowl with the turkey. Add the tomatoes, cucumber, onion, vinegar, mint, cumin, the remaining 2 tablespoons oil, and the remaining $^1/_4$ teaspoon salt and $^1/_8$ teaspoon pepper. Toss to mix.

What's for Lunch

 Finish with a bunch of grapes and cheese—try a sharp Greek goat's milk cheese flavored with herbs or sun-dried tomatoes.

 COOK'S TIP Many markets now stock turkey breast cutlets precut into strips, making preparation of this simple salad entrée even easier.

8 POINTS per serving

Per serving:
367 Calories • 11 g Total Fat • 2 g Saturated Fat • 70 mg Cholesterol • 597 mg Sodium • 33 mg Total Carbohydrate
3 g Dietary Fiber • 33 g Protein • 78 mg Calcium

Cuban Sandwiches

Currently showing up on menus everywhere, Cuban sandwiches are all the rage—and once you take a bite you'll understand why. In restaurants, they are made with a commercial sandwich press, but for our homemade version we use a heavy skillet to "press" them down.

Makes 4 servings

2 tablespoons mustard

8 ounces French bread (about $1/2$ baguette), split open

$1/4$ pound reduced-fat deli-sliced Swiss cheese

$1/4$ pound deli-sliced turkey

$1/4$ pound deli-sliced ham

12 slices dill pickle

1 Spread the mustard over the inside of the baguette. Layer the bottom half of the baguette with the cheese, turkey, and ham. Arrange the pickles on top. Cover with the top and cut in half into 2 sandwiches.

2 Heat a large nonstick skillet over medium heat and spray with nonstick cooking spray. Add the sandwiches and place a heavy skillet on top, pressing down to flatten them. Cook 3 minutes, remove the top skillet, and turn the sandwiches over. Press down again with the skillet. Cook until the cheese melts and the sandwiches are heated through, 4–5 minutes. Cut each sandwich in half crosswise before serving.

What's for Lunch

To keep the Cuban theme, serve with a black bean salad

COOK'S TIP To flatten the sandwiches, it's best to use a heavy skillet, such as cast-iron, that is slightly smaller than the skillet in which the sandwiches are cooked.

6 *POINTS* per serving

Per serving:
291 Calories • 8 g Total Fat • 4 g Saturated Fat • 38 mg Cholesterol • 1,100 mg Sodium • 31 mg Total Carbohydrate
2 g Dietary Fiber • 23 g Protein • 250 mg Calcium

Sausage and Bean Soup

The perfect soup to take the chill off a winter afternoon, Polish-style kielbasa gives this hearty soup its intense flavor. Be sure to choose turkey kielbasa, which has two-thirds less fat than the traditional pork or beef variety.

*Makes 6 servings
(yield 8 cups)*

1 teaspoon canola oil

1/2 pound turkey kielbasa, cut into 1/2-inch cubes

1/2 cup chopped onion

2 small carrots, chopped

1 celery stalk, chopped

4 cups reduced-sodium chicken broth

1 (15-ounce) can pinto beans, rinsed and drained

1 (10-ounce) package frozen chopped spinach, thawed and squeezed dry

Heat the oil in a large nonstick saucepan. Add the kielbasa and saute until lightly browned, about 3 minutes. Add the onion, carrots, celery, broth, and beans; bring to a boil. Cover, reduce the heat, and simmer until the vegetables are tender, about 10 minutes. Add the spinach and continue to cook until heated through, about 2 minutes.

What's for Lunch

Soft bread sticks and a chilled beer complement this satisfying soup deliciously.

 COOK'S TIP This soup can be made up to three days ahead and refrigerated, which allows the flavors a chance to develop. Make sure you reheat it thoroughly, bringing the soup to a boil and simmering it for five minutes.

3 *POINTS* per serving

Per serving:
157 Calories • 4 g Total Fat • 1 g Saturated Fat • 23 mg Cholesterol • 988 mg Sodium • 16 mg Total Carbohydrate
5 g Dietary Fiber • 13 g Protein • 87 mg Calcium

Turkey Sausage Fajitas

If you tend to shy away from Mexican food, then try our svelte rendition of these succulent fajitas, made with lean turkey sausage.

Makes 4 servings

1 teaspoon canola oil

1/2 pound Italian-style turkey sausage, cut into 1/2-inch slices

2 green bell peppers, seeded and thinly sliced

1 large onion, thinly sliced

4 (8-inch) low-fat flour tortillas, warmed

1 Heat the oil in a large nonstick skillet. Add the sausage and saute until browned, about 5 minutes. Add the peppers and onion; cover and cook until the vegetables are tender and the sausage is cooked through, about 10 minutes.

2 Spoon the sausage mixture down the center of each tortilla and roll the tortilla up around the filling.

What's for Lunch

Garnish the fajitas with sliced tomatoes, tomatillos (Mexican green tomatoes), and pickled peppers.

COOK'S TIP An easy way to heat tortillas is to loosely wrap them in microwavable plastic wrap and heat in a microwave oven on High for one minute. To keep them soft and warm, cover the warm tortillas until ready to serve. If you're really a Mexican food fan, look in your favorite kitchenware store for a tortilla warmer.

Per serving:
227 Calories • 7 g Total Fat • 2 g Saturated Fat • 30 mg Cholesterol • 718 mg Sodium • 29 mg Total Carbohydrate • 11 g Dietary Fiber • 13 g Protein • 57 mg Calcium

4 POINTS per serving

LUNCH

Grilled Lamb Burgers with Lemon-Garlic Mayonnaise

Lamb burgers are a rich, robust change of pace from the typical hamburger. Take care not to overcook the burgers, or the lamb could become dry. Here we serve them with a seasoned mayonnaise that's a takeoff of aïoli, the pungent garlic mayonnaise beloved by the French.

Makes 4 servings

1¹/₄ pounds lean ground lamb

¹/₄ cup minced onion

1 teaspoon dried oregano

¹/₂ teaspoon salt

¹/₄ teaspoon coarsely ground black pepper

¹/₄ cup reduced-calorie mayonnaise

1 garlic clove, minced

1 teaspoon grated lemon zest

1 teaspoon fresh lemon juice

1 tablespoon chopped fresh mint

4 hamburger rolls, split open

4 green-leaf lettuce leaves

2 tomatoes, sliced

1 Mix the lamb, onion, oregano, salt, and pepper in a bowl. Shape into 4 burgers. Spray a nonstick, ridged grill pan with nonstick spray and heat the griddle over medium–high heat. Cook the burgers until browned on the outside and done to taste, 3–4 minutes on each side for medium–rare.

2 Meanwhile, mix the mayonnaise, garlic, lemon zest, lemon juice, and mint in a small bowl. Spread the mayonnaise mixture on the buns. Lay a lettuce leaf in each, add a burger, and top with tomato slices.

What's for Lunch

Dress up the burgers with a relish assortment, including dill pickles, raw cucumber wedges, carrot sticks, and scallions.

COOK'S TIP Low-fat cooking is easy with the variety of nonstick pans now on the market. With nonstick, ridged grill pans, you can grill on your stovetop year-round. The larger, two-burner grill pans are perfect for grilling meat and vegetables at the same time.

8 POINTS per serving

Per serving:
381 Calories • 13 g Total Fat • 4 g Saturated Fat • 107 mg Cholesterol • 755 mg Sodium • 27 mg Total Carbohydrate 3 g Dietary Fiber • 36 g Protein • 97 mg Calcium

Grilled Lamb Burgers with Lemon-Garlic Mayonnaise

Southwestern Skillet Macaroni and Cheese

You can adjust the spice level of this healthy take on a perennial favorite according to taste. Chock-full of ground meat, chili powder and cumin, it's a cross between classic Southern mac-and-cheese and Tex-Mex chili.

*Makes 6 servings
(yield 6 cups)*

1 cup elbow macaroni

1 pound ground skinless turkey breast

1/2 cup chopped onion

1/2 cup seeded and chopped green bell pepper

2 tablespoons chili powder

1 teaspoon ground cumin

1/2 teaspoon salt

1 (14 1/2-ounce) can diced tomatoes, with their juice

1 (8-ounce) can tomato sauce

1 (4 1/2-ounce) can chopped mild green chiles

1/2 cup water

1 cup shredded reduced-fat cheddar cheese (preferably extra sharp)

1 Bring a pot of water to a boil. Cook the macaroni according to package directions; drain and keep warm.

2 Spray a large nonstick skillet with nonstick spray. Add the turkey and cook until no longer pink, stirring with a wooden spoon to break up the meat. Stir in the onion, bell pepper, chili powder, cumin, and salt. Cook, stirring occasionally, until the onion is tender, about 3 minutes. Add the tomatoes, tomato sauce, chiles, and water; simmer, uncovered, 10 minutes. Add the macaroni and the cheese, stirring to combine.

What's for Lunch

Serve with an assortment of garnishes from which your family can choose, including diced white onion, sliced jalapeño pepper, light sour cream, and crushed baked tortilla chips.

6 POINTS per serving

Per serving:
297 Calories • 13 g Total Fat • 5 g Saturated Fat • 73 mg Cholesterol • 1,053 mg Sodium • 22 mg Total Carbohydrate
3 g Dietary Fiber • 22 g Protein • 198 mg Calcium

Soba Noodles with Tofu in Ginger Broth

Soba is a Japanese noodle made from buckwheat and wheat flour. It has a distinctive grayish-brown color and can usually be found in the Asian section of your market. Like most Japanese noodles, it is extremely low in fat.

Makes 4 servings (yield 5 cups)

1/2 pound soba noodles

4 cups fat-free, reduced-sodium chicken broth

6 quarter-size slices unpeeled fresh ginger

1 teaspoon reduced-sodium soy sauce

1 teaspoon Asian (dark) sesame oil

1/2 pound firm tofu, cut into 1-inch chunks

2 cups sliced mushrooms

2 large scallions, chopped

1 Bring a large pot of salted water to a boil. Cook the noodles according to package directions; drain.

2 Meanwhile, combine the broth, ginger, soy sauce, and oil in a medium saucepan over medium-high heat. Bring to a boil, cover, reduce the heat, and simmer 5 minutes. Stir in the tofu and mushrooms, re-cover, and cook 5 minutes longer. Remove from the heat and stir in the scallions.

3 Place 3/4 cup soba noodles in each of 4 bowls and top with the tofu mixture.

What's for Dinner

Broccoli florets, stir-fried with crushed garlic, make a lovely side dish to serve with this tofu dish.

COOK'S TIP Chunks of unpeeled fresh ginger lend the broth a robust flavor, but are too bitter to be eaten; discard just before serving.

5 *POINTS* per serving

Per serving (1 1/4 cups):
275 Calories • 4 g Total Fat • 1 g Saturated Fat • 0 mg Cholesterol • 1,129 mg Sodium • 47 mg Total Carbohydrate
3 g Dietary Fiber • 17 g Protein • 138 mg Calcium

Cheese and Pinto Bean Tostadas

Makes 4 servings

8 (6-inch) reduced-fat corn tortillas

2 teaspoons vegetable oil

1 garlic clove, minced

1 small onion, chopped

1 (15-ounce) can pinto beans, rinsed and drained

1 (7-ounce) can corn, drained, or 3/4 cup thawed frozen corn kernels

1 teaspoon ground cumin

1 cup tomato salsa

2 tablespoons chopped cilantro

1/2 cup shredded reduced-fat sharp cheddar cheese

4 tablespoons nonfat sour cream

Tostadas are traditionally made by frying tortillas in oil until crisp. By baking the tortillas, we cut much of the fat out of this recipe without losing flavor. Use any salsa of your choice, but the fire-roasted varieties will deliver the most flavor.

1 Preheat the oven to 450°F. Place the tortillas in a single layer on a baking sheet and bake until crisp, 8–10 minutes.

2 Heat the oil in a large nonstick skillet over medium–high heat. Add the garlic and onion; cook until they begin to soften, about 2 minutes. Add the beans, corn, and cumin; cook, stirring occasionally, 4–5 minutes. Stir in the salsa and cook 2 minutes longer. Remove from the heat and stir in the cilantro.

3 For each serving, spread 2/3 cup of the bean mixture on a tortilla. Top with 2 tablespoons of the cheese and cover with a second tortilla. Garnish with 1 tablespoon of the sour cream.

What's for Dinner

  Serve the tostadas with a mixed green salad of loose leaf lettuce, frisee, and radicchio, tossed with a light lime dressing.

 COOK'S TIP To make a light lime dressing, mix two teaspoons each of fresh lime juice, chicken broth, and extra-virgin olive oil. Season with one-half teaspoon honey, and salt and pepper to taste.

6 POINTS per serving

Per serving:
287 Calories • 7 g Total Fat • 2 g Saturated Fat • 8 mg Cholesterol • 825 mg Sodium • 43 mg Total Carbohydrate
9 g Dietary Fiber • 13 g Protein • 307 mg Calcium

Penne with Asparagus and Parmesan

Ziti works as well as penne in this versatile dish. When fresh tomatoes are in season, you can add two chopped ripe tomatoes in place of the canned tomatoes.

Makes 4 servings

1/2 pound penne

1 tablespoon olive oil

1 garlic clove, thinly sliced

1 (14 1/2-ounce) can diced tomatoes, with their juice

1/2 cup reduced-sodium chicken broth

1 pound asparagus, cut on the diagonal into 1-inch pieces

1/2 cup coarsely chopped fresh basil

1/4 cup grated Parmesan cheese

1 Bring a large pot of water to a boil. Cook the penne according to package directions; drain and keep warm in the pot.

2 Meanwhile, heat the oil in a large skillet over medium-low heat. Add the garlic; cook just until it begins to turn golden. Add the tomatoes and broth and bring to a boil. Reduce the heat and simmer, uncovered, 5 minutes. Add the asparagus; cover and simmer until tender, about 5 minutes longer; pour over the penne. Add the basil and Parmesan cheese; toss to coat.

What's for Dinner

For a satisfying, yet light, dinner broiled tilapia or orange roughy would be delicious.

6 *POINTS* per serving

Per serving:
302 Calories • 6 g Total Fat • 2 g Saturated Fat • 4 mg Cholesterol • 582 mg Sodium • 48 mg Total Carbohydrate
3 g Dietary Fiber • 13 g Protein • 100 mg Calcium

Pasta with Roasted Red Pepper Sauce

In this dish we've created a creamy (guilt-free!) roasted pepper sauce, made with fat-free half-and-half available in markets across the country.

*Makes 4 servings
(yield 2 cups sauce)*

1/2 pound pasta

1 teaspoon olive oil

1/2 cup chopped onion

1 garlic clove, minced

1 (12-ounce) jar roasted red peppers, drained and chopped

1 cup coarsely chopped fresh basil

3/4 cup reduced-sodium chicken broth

1/4 cup fat-free half-and-half

1 Bring a large pot of water to a boil. Add the pasta and cook according to package directions. Drain and keep warm.

2 Meanwhile, heat the oil in a nonstick saucepan over medium–low heat. Add the onion and garlic; cook until the onion is soft, about 5 minutes. Stir in the roasted peppers and basil; cook about 1 minute longer to allow the flavors to blend. Add the broth; simmer, uncovered, 10 minutes longer. Remove from the heat and stir in the half-and-half.

3 Puree the sauce in a food processor or blender. Pour the sauce over the pasta and toss to coat.

What's for Dinner

 This dish is spectacular served with grilled zucchini slices.

 COOK'S TIP Basil lovers can double the amount of basil called for in this recipe. Since the sauce is pureed, you won't need to chop the basil.

5 POINTS per serving

Per serving:
258 Calories • 2 g Total Fat • 0 g Saturated Fat • 0 mg Cholesterol • 244 mg Sodium • 50 mg Total Carbohydrate
3 g Dietary Fiber • 9 g Protein • 51 mg Calcium

Pasta with Roasted Red Pepper Sauce

Catfish with Salsa Verde

Drizzled with a fresh-tasting green sauce and sprinkled with Cajun seasoning, these catfish fillets are definitely on the spicy side. Here, they're served on a pretty base of yellow and red tomatoes, perfect for entertaining.

Makes 4 servings

1 cup cilantro leaves

1/4 cup fresh parsley leaves

2 tablespoons capers, drained

3 tablespoons cider vinegar

2 tablespoons reduced-sodium chicken broth

1 1/2 tablespoons olive oil

4 (6-ounce) catfish fillets

1 tablespoon Cajun seasoning

8 slices red tomato

8 slices yellow tomato

1 Puree the cilantro, parsley, capers, vinegar, broth, and 1 tablespoon of the olive oil in a blender or food processor.

2 Sprinkle the catfish with the Cajun seasoning. Heat the remaining 1/2 tablespoon oil in a large nonstick skillet over medium-high heat. Add the catfish and cook until just opaque in the center, about 3 minutes on each side.

3 Arrange the yellow and red tomato slices on 4 plates, top with the fillets, and drizzle with the sauce.

What's for Dinner

 Consider serving the fish with plain, boiled new potatoes to tame the dish's heat.

 COOK'S TIP Yellow tomatoes are slightly less acidic than red, and have a sweet, mild flavor. If you prefer, simply use all yellow slices in this dish.

6 *POINTS* per serving

Per serving:
257 Calories • 15 g Total Fat • 3 g Saturated Fat • 82 mg Cholesterol • 672 mg Sodium • 6 mg Total Carbohydrate 2 g Dietary Fiber • 25 g Protein • 37 mg Calcium

Capellini with Clams and a Tomato-Feta Vinaigrette

Think of this delightfully different pasta dish as a warm salad served over capellini, a delicate pasta just a bit thicker than angel's hair. You could easily substitute vermicelli, if you like.

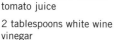

Makes 4 servings (yield 8 cups)

1/2 pound capellini

1 (10-ounce) can whole baby clams, drained

1/4 pound feta cheese, crumbled

3/4 cup reduced-sodium tomato juice

2 tablespoons white wine vinegar

1 tablespoon extra-virgin olive oil

1/2 teaspoon salt

1/4 teaspoon coarsely ground black pepper

3 plum tomatoes, chopped

3/4 cup chopped fresh basil

1/2 cup chopped fresh parsley

 1 Bring a large pot of salted water to a boil. Add the capellini and cook according to package directions. Add the clams for the last 30 seconds of cooking; drain and transfer to a large bowl.

2 Meanwhile, combine the feta cheese, tomato juice, vinegar, oil, salt, and pepper in a bowl. Pour over the pasta and clams. Add the tomatoes, basil, and parsley; toss to combine.

What's for Dinner

All you need to add to satisfy the family is hot garlic bread.

 COOK'S TIP Use Bulgarian feta cheese if you're lucky enough to find it; it has a sharper flavor than the Greek variety.

9 POINTS per serving

Per serving:
428 Calories • 12 g Total Fat • 5 g Saturated Fat • 63 mg Cholesterol • 839 mg Sodium • 52 mg Total Carbohydrate
3 g Dietary Fiber • 27 g Protein • 231 mg Calcium

DINNER

Flounder Oreganata

Oregano is the primary flavor in the tasty bread-crumb topping, which also works well on any mild white fish such as snapper, halibut, or cod. You could also try the topping as stuffing for mushrooms, baked clams, or tomatoes.

Makes 4 servings

4 (6-ounce) flounder fillets

2 tablespoons olive oil

³/₄ cup plain dried bread crumbs

¹/₄ cup chopped fresh parsley

3 tablespoons fresh lemon juice

1 garlic clove, minced

¹/₄ teaspoon salt

¹/₄ teaspoon dried oregano

1 Preheat the oven to 425°F. Coat a baking sheet with nonstick spray.

2 Place the fish fillets on the baking sheet. Combine the olive oil, bread crumbs, parsley, lemon juice, garlic, salt, and oregano in a bowl. Press an equal amount of the bread crumb mixture onto the top of each fillet. Bake until the fish is just opaque in the center, about 10 minutes.

What's for Dinner

 Serve the fish with a quick-cooking rice pilaf and steamed green beans.

COOK'S TIP A squeeze of fresh lemon juice and a few toasted sliced almonds will liven up the green beans.

7 POINTS per serving

Per serving:
303 Calories • 10 g Total Fat • 2 g Saturated Fat • 92 mg Cholesterol • 464 mg Sodium • 16 mg Total Carbohydrate
1 g Dietary Fiber • 35 g Protein • 79 mg Calcium

Citrus-Scented Halibut

Halibut is a firm-fleshed fish that has a mild flavor. It's low in fat and available year-round, but is especially plentiful from March through September. In this recipe, it is teamed with a refreshing citrus sauce.

Makes 4 servings

3 tablespoons orange juice

2 tablespoons fresh lemon juice

1 tablespoon reduced-sodium soy sauce

1 teaspoon grated orange zest

1 teaspoon grated lemon zest

$\frac{1}{2}$ teaspoon salt

$\frac{1}{4}$ teaspoon coarsely ground black pepper

2 (12-ounce) halibut steaks

2 navel oranges, peeled and separated into segments, juice reserved

 Preheat the broiler. Coat the rack of a broiler pan with nonstick spray.

 Combine the orange juice, lemon juice, soy sauce, orange zest, lemon zest, salt, and pepper in a large bowl. Add the halibut steaks and marinate 7 minutes, turning occasionally.

3 Place the steaks on the broiler pan and broil, 3 inches from the heat, until just opaque in the center, 3–4 minutes on each side. Cut each steak in half, top with the orange segments, and drizzle with the reserved juice.

What's for Dinner

We suggest serving this dinner with large grain, pearl-like Israeli couscous, which works nicely with assertive citrus-based sauces.

4 POINTS per serving

Per serving:
217 Calories • 4 g Total Fat • 1 g Saturated Fat • 52 mg Cholesterol • 302 mg Sodium • 9 mg Total Carbohydrate
2 g Dietary Fiber • 35 g Protein • 107 mg Calcium

Peppered Sea Bass with Fresh Herb Sauce

Makes 4 servings

4 (6-ounce) sea bass fillets

3/4 teaspoon coarsely ground black pepper

3/4 teaspoon salt

1/4 cup parsley leaves

1/4 cup cilantro leaves

1/4 cup mint leaves

1 garlic clove, chopped

3 tablespoons cider vinegar

2 tablespoons reduced-sodium chicken broth

2 tablespoons extra-virgin olive oil

This hearty seafood dish sports a luscious peppery crust that is typically used in the French classic, steak au poivre. The fresh herb sauce, with which it is served, works equally well with many other types of fish, as well as with chicken or lamb.

 1 Sprinkle both sides of the sea bass with the pepper and 1/2 teaspoon of the salt. Spray a large heavy nonstick skillet with nonstick spray; heat over medium–high heat. Cook the bass until a crust has formed on the outside and the fish is just opaque in the center, about 3 minutes on each side. Transfer to a plate and let rest 5 minutes.

2 Meanwhile, puree the parsley, cilantro, mint, garlic, vinegar, broth, oil, and the remaining 1/4 teaspoon salt in a food processor or blender. Spoon the sauce over the bass.

What's for Dinner

The dish is great with quinoa, an extraordinarily healthy South American grain readily available in many supermarkets.

 COOK'S TIP Quinoa must be rinsed to remove its natural bitter coating. Then cook one cup quinoa in two cups chicken broth or water for 20 minutes.

---

5 *POINTS* per serving

Per serving:
229 Calories • 10 g Total Fat • 2 g Saturated Fat • 68 mg Cholesterol • 571 mg Sodium • 2 mg Total Carbohydrate
1 g Dietary Fiber • 31 g Protein • 41 mg Calcium

Sea Bass with Dill Couscous

Chilean sea bass is a meaty, richly flavored fish that is low in fat. It is elegant on its own, or, as it is served here, paired with an exotic Mediterranean herbed pasta.

Makes 4 servings

1 teaspoon ground cumin

¹/₂ teaspoon ground coriander

¹/₂ teaspoon ground cinnamon

1 teaspoon salt

¹/₂ teaspoon coarsely ground black pepper

4 (6-ounce) Chilean sea bass fillets

2 teaspoons olive oil

1 onion, chopped

1 pint cherry tomatoes, halved

1 tablespoon capers, drained

3 tablespoons fresh lemon juice

1³/₄ cups water

1¹/₂ cups quick-cooking couscous

1 red bell pepper, seeded and chopped

3 tablespoons chopped fresh mint

2 tablespoons chopped fresh dill

 1 Combine the cumin, coriander, cinnamon, ¹/₄ teaspoon of the salt, and ¹/₈ teaspoon of the black pepper in a bowl. Sprinkle the mixture over the fish fillets. Heat the oil in a large nonstick skillet over medium-high heat. Add the fish, skin-side up, and cook 5 minutes. Turn the fillets over and cook until just opaque in the center, about 5 minutes longer. Transfer the fish to a plate and cover to keep warm.

2 Add the onion and tomatoes to the skillet and cook 3 minutes. Add the capers, 1 tablespoon of the lemon juice, ¹/₄ teaspoon of the salt, and ¹/₈ teaspoon of the pepper; cook 1 minute longer and remove from the heat.

3 Meanwhile, bring the water to a boil in a saucepan. Remove the pan from the heat; stir in the couscous, bell pepper, and the remaining ¹/₂ teaspoon salt and ¹/₄ teaspoon black pepper. Cover and let stand until the water is absorbed, about 5 minutes; stir in the mint, dill, and the remaining 2 tablespoons lemon juice. Spoon the tomato mixture over the fish and serve the couscous alongside.

What's for Dinner

Serve the fish and couscous with steamed baby spinach.

Per serving:
493 Calories • 7 g Total Fat • 1 g Saturated Fat • 70 mg Cholesterol • 780 mg Sodium • 64 mg Total Carbohydrate
7 g Dietary Fiber • 42 g Protein • 68 mg Calcium

Sesame-Glazed Shrimp with Snow Peas and Baby Corn

Quick and easy, yet festive enough for company, this colorful shrimp and vegetable stir-fry boasts an aromatic mixture of Asian sauces laced with sherry and honey.

Makes 4 servings (yield 5 cups)

2 tablespoons hoisin sauce

2 tablespoons reduced-sodium soy sauce

2 tablespoons sherry

1 tablespoon honey

2 teaspoons cornstarch

1 tablespoon Asian (dark) sesame oil

1 1/2 pounds large shrimp, peeled and deveined

1 tablespoon grated peeled fresh ginger

1 garlic clove, minced

2 large scallions, chopped

1/2 pound snow peas, trimmed

1 (8-ounce) can baby corn, drained

2 teaspoons sesame seeds

1 Combine the hoisin sauce, soy sauce, sherry, honey, and cornstarch in a small bowl.

2 Heat 2 teaspoons of the oil in a large nonstick skillet over medium-high heat. Add the shrimp and stir-fry until pink, 3–4 minutes; transfer the shrimp to a bowl. To the skillet, add the remaining 1 teaspoon oil, the ginger, garlic, and scallions; stir-fry 30 seconds. Add the snow peas and baby corn and stir-fry until the snow peas are bright green, about 3 minutes. Stir in the hoisin mixture and the reserved shrimp. Bring to a boil and cook, stirring occasionally, until thickened, 1–2 minutes. Remove from the heat and stir in the sesame seeds.

What's for Dinner

Spoon the stir-fry over a quick-to-prepare low-fat Asian noodle, such as rice stick vermicelli.

 COOK'S TIP If you prefer, you can substitute an equal amount of water for the sherry.

132

6 POINTS per serving

Per serving (1 1/4 cups):
286 Calories • 7 g Total Fat • 1 g Saturated Fat • 210 mg Cholesterol • 763 mg Sodium • 21 mg Total Carbohydrate
5 g Dietary Fiber • 32 g Protein • 127 mg Calcium

Sesame-Glazed Shrimp with Snow Peas and Baby Corn

Sweet and Sour Shrimp

Sweet and sour dishes, which derive their distinctive taste from deep frying and a vinegar-and-sugar sauce, have long been popular in Chinese cuisine. Since the shrimp in this version are stir-fried in a modest amount of oil, we've added peanuts for extra flavor and crunch.

**Makes 4 servings
(yield 5 cups)**

³/4 cup pineapple juice

3 tablespoons sugar

3 tablespoons rice vinegar

2 tablespoons tomato paste

1 tablespoon reduced-sodium soy sauce

1 tablespoon cornstarch

2 dashes hot pepper sauce

1 tablespoon vegetable oil

1¹/2 pounds medium shrimp, peeled and deveined

1 tablespoon grated peeled fresh ginger

2 garlic cloves, minced

2 carrots, very thinly sliced

1 onion, chopped

1 green bell pepper, seeded and chopped

1 (8-ounce) can bamboo shoots, drained

¹/4 cup roasted peanuts

1 Combine the pineapple juice, sugar, vinegar, tomato paste, soy sauce, cornstarch, and pepper sauce in a bowl.

2 Heat 2 teaspoons of the oil in a large nonstick skillet over medium-high heat. Add the shrimp and stir-fry until pink, 3–4 minutes. Transfer the shrimp to a bowl. To the skillet, add the remaining 1 teaspoon oil, the ginger, and garlic and stir-fry 30 seconds. Add the carrots, onion, bell pepper, bamboo shoots, and peanuts; stir-fry until the vegetables begin to soften, 4–5 minutes. Stir in the reserved shrimp and the pineapple juice mixture. Bring to a boil and cook, stirring constantly, until thickened, about 2 minutes.

What's for Dinner

Sweet and sour dishes go particularly well with jasmine rice, an aromatic Thai rice now stocked in many supermarkets.

COOK'S TIP The trick to successful stir-frying is to have all your ingredients prepared before you start cooking and to cook the food over a relatively high heat. Try holding a wooden spatula in each hand and continuously push the food up from the bottom of the pan and over.

7 POINTS per serving

Per serving:
358 Calories • 11 g Total Fat • 1 g Saturated Fat • 210 mg Cholesterol • 439 mg Sodium • 33 g Total Carbohydrate • 4 g Dietary Fiber • 33 g Protein • 112 mg Calcium

Sesame-Crusted Swordfish with Scallions

Makes 4 servings

3 tablespoons reduced-sodium soy sauce

3 tablespoons red wine vinegar

2 tablespoons honey

1 tablespoon Asian (dark) sesame oil

2 teaspoons arrowroot

1/4 teaspoon crushed red pepper

4 (6-ounce) swordfish steaks, about 3/4-inch thick

1/2 teaspoon salt

1/4 teaspoon coarsely ground black pepper

6 tablespoons sesame seeds

2 teaspoons canola oil

4 scallions, thinly sliced on the diagonal

Arrowroot, which comes from a tropical tuber, is the thickener used for the scallion sauce to finish these flavorful swordfish steaks. It can be found in the baking section of your market, and becomes clear when cooked. If you can't find it, substitute one tablespoon cornstarch.

1 Combine the soy sauce, vinegar, honey, oil, arrowroot, and crushed red pepper in a bowl.

2 Sprinkle the swordfish with the salt and black pepper, then sprinkle with the sesame seeds, pressing the seeds onto both sides of each steak.

3 Heat the oil in a large nonstick skillet over medium-high heat. Cook the swordfish until done to taste, about 3 minutes on each side for medium; transfer to a platter. Add the soy sauce mixture and scallions to the skillet. Bring almost to a boil and cook, stirring occasionally, until the sauce just begins to thicken, about 2 minutes. Spoon the sauce over the swordfish.

What's for Dinner

We suggest you team this dish with a stir fry of mixed vegetables and rice.

COOK'S TIP Sesame seeds are best stored in the freezer where they will stay fresh and ready to use for months.

9 POINTS per serving

Per serving:
389 Calories • 19 g Total Fat • 3 g Saturated Fat • 66 mg Cholesterol • 855 mg Sodium • 16 mg Total Carbohydrate 2 g Dietary Fiber • 38 g Protein • 153 mg Calcium

Pan-Seared Tuna Niçoise

Redolent of the flavors of the South of France—tomatoes, olives, garlic, anchovies, and capers—this simple, yet elegant dinner is sure to delight. It is a warm and filling version of the cold tuna salad so popular in France.

Makes 4 servings

3 plum tomatoes, chopped

$^1/_2$ cup finely chopped red onion

$^1/_4$ cup pitted and chopped kalamata olives

$^1/_4$ cup coarsely chopped fresh basil

2 tablespoons capers, drained

2 anchovy fillets, rinsed, patted dry, and minced

1 garlic clove, minced

1 tablespoon extra-virgin olive oil

4 (6-ounce) tuna steaks

1 teaspoon dried thyme

$^1/_2$ teaspoon salt

$^1/_2$ teaspoon coarsely ground black pepper

1 Combine the tomatoes, onion, olives, basil, capers, anchovies, garlic, and oil in a bowl.

2 Sprinkle the tuna steaks with the thyme, salt, and pepper. Heat a large nonstick skillet over high heat; spray with nonstick spray. Add the tuna and cook until browned on the outside and pink in the center, about 3 minutes on each side for medium-rare. Remove from the heat and spoon the tomato mixture over the steaks.

What's for Dinner

 Team the fish with a side of sauteed kale.

 COOK'S TIP Rinsing the anchovies helps reduce the amount of salt in the recipe. Remember to pat them dry with a paper towel before using to absorb excess water.

136   **5 *POINTS* per serving**

Per serving:
247 Calories • 6 g Total Fat • 1 g Saturated Fat • 76 mg Cholesterol • 632 mg Sodium • 6 mg Total Carbohydrate 2 g Dietary Fiber • 40 g Protein • 61 mg Calcium

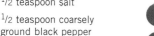
Zesty Chicken with Shallots, Capers, and Olives

Makes 4 servings

1 pound thin-sliced skin-less boneless chicken breasts

1 teaspoon dried rosemary, crumbled

$1/2$ teaspoon salt

$1/2$ teaspoon coarsely ground black pepper

2 teaspoons olive oil

2 shallots, chopped

1 garlic clove, minced

3 tablespoons cider vinegar

$1/4$ cup dry white wine

1 ($14^1/2$ ounce) can diced tomatoes, with their juice

5 kalamata olives, pitted and chopped

1 tablespoon capers, drained

$1/4$ cup chopped fresh basil

The spicy tomato sauce in this dish—redolent of garlic, rosemary, and basil—looks and smells as though you slaved for hours. Be sure not to drain the diced tomatoes; you will need the extra liquid their juice will provide.

1 Sprinkle the chicken with the rosemary, salt, and pepper.

2 Heat the oil in a large nonstick skillet over medium-high heat. Sauté the chicken until browned and cooked through, about 3 minutes on each side; transfer to a plate. Add the shallots and garlic to the skillet and cook until the shallots are soft, about 1 minute. Stir in the vinegar; continue to cook until the vinegar evaporates, about 30 seconds. Add the wine, tomatoes, olives, and capers. Simmer, uncovered, until the sauce thickens slightly, about 8 minutes. Stir in the basil. Return the chicken to the skillet and cook about 1 minute longer to heat through.

What's for Dinner

Serve the chicken over your favorite thin-strand pasta with a tossed green salad on the side.

COOK'S TIP
Look for chicken breasts labeled "thin-cut"; for the best results, you want breasts about $1/4$-inch thick.

4 POINTS per serving

Per serving:
186 Calories • 4 g Total Fat • 1 g Saturated Fat • 66 mg Cholesterol • 878 mg Sodium • 8 mg Total Carbohydrate
1 g Dietary Fiber • 28 g Protein • 34 mg Calcium

Chicken and Ham "Pot Pie"

Topped with a buttermilk biscuit crust and served in the cooking skillet, this is an incredibly easy alternative to usually time-consuming pot pie. Dinner guests will love the presentation, but this one-pot recipe is so simple it's a shame not to try it at the end of a hectic workday. The chicken thighs are moist and flavorful, but if you can't find skinless boneless thighs in your market, substitute chicken breasts if you prefer.

Makes 8 servings

1 (7½-ounce) package refrigerated buttermilk biscuits

1 tablespoon butter

1 pound skinless boneless chicken thighs, trimmed of all visible fat and cut into 1-inch cubes

1 (8-ounce) ham steak, cut into ½-inch cubes

2 garlic cloves, minced

1 onion, chopped

1 (10-ounce) package frozen mixed vegetables

1 cup fat-free, reduced-sodium chicken broth

1 teaspoon dried thyme

½ teaspoon coarsely ground black pepper

2 tablespoons cornstarch

¾ cup low-fat (2%) milk

 Preheat the oven to 400°F. Prepare the biscuits according to package directions.

Meanwhile, melt the butter in a large nonstick skillet over medium-high heat. Add the chicken and ham; cook, stirring occasionally, until the chicken is almost cooked through, about 6 minutes. Add the garlic, onion, and mixed vegetables. Cook, stirring occasionally, until the vegetables are tender, about 4 minutes. Stir in the broth, thyme, and pepper; cook 2 minutes.

Blend the cornstarch with the milk in a small bowl, and stir into the skillet. Bring the mixture to a boil and cook, stirring constantly until thickened, about 1 minute. Top the skillet with the biscuits and serve.

What's for Dinner

 Serve the pot pie with a mixed green salad.

COOK'S TIP If you aren't able to find refrigerated buttermilk biscuits, substitute an equal amount of the brown-and-serve type rolls usually stocked in the market's bread aisle.

5 POINTS per serving

Per serving:
225 Calories • 6 g Total Fat • 2 g Saturated Fat • 68 mg Cholesterol • 760 mg Sodium • 22 mg Total Carbohydrate • 2 g Dietary Fiber • 20 g Protein • 53 mg Calcium

Chicken and Ham "Pot Pie"

DINNER

Chili-Spiked Rice and Bean Salad with Chicken

*Makes 6 servings
(yield 6 cups)*

4 cups cooked boil-in-bag rice

3 tablespoons chopped fresh parsley

2 tablespoons cider vinegar

2 tablespoons extra-virgin olive oil

1 tablespoon chili powder

$1/2$ teaspoon salt

$1/2$ teaspoon ground cumin

2 cups cubed cooked chicken breast

1 (15-ounce) can red kidney beans, rinsed and drained

$1/2$ cup seeded and chopped green bell pepper

2 large scallions, chopped

This zesty rice salad holds up well as a buffet item; to feed a crowd, just double the ingredients. You could use quick-cooking rice, but this recipe is so speedy that you have time to make the somewhat fluffier boil-in-bag variety.

Combine the rice, parsley, vinegar, oil, chili powder, salt, and cumin in a large bowl. Stir in the chicken, beans, bell pepper, and scallions; toss to combine.

What's for Dinner

Pureed squash (available in the frozen food section of your market) makes a delicious side dish.

COOK'S TIP If you're in a pinch, you can pick up the rice from your favorite Chinese take-out on your way home from work. If you have any leftovers, freeze the rice, right in its container, inside a zip-close bag.

140

9 POINTS per serving

Per serving:
459 Calories • 8 g Total Fat • 1 g Saturated Fat • 40 mg Cholesterol • 500 mg Sodium • 75 mg Total Carbohydrate
7 g Dietary Fiber • 24 g Protein • 37 mg Calcium

Turkey Cutlets with Cranberry-Pear Chutney

This easy-to-make chutney goes well with chicken or pork, as well as with turkey. If you're really pressed for time, use one small can of drained pears instead of fresh pear.

Makes 4 servings

6 tablespoons packed light brown sugar

1/4 cup reduced-sodium chicken broth

1/4 cup cider vinegar

2 tablespoons orange juice

1/4 teaspoon ground cinnamon

1/4 teaspoon ground ginger

Pinch of ground cloves

4 (4-ounce) turkey cutlets

1/2 teaspoon salt

1/4 teaspoon coarsely ground black pepper

1 teaspoon canola oil

1 ripe pear, peeled, cored, and chopped

1 cup fresh or frozen cranberries

1 Whisk together the brown sugar, broth, vinegar, orange juice, cinnamon, ginger, and cloves in a small bowl.

2 Sprinkle the turkey cutlets with the salt and pepper. Heat the oil in a large nonstick skillet over medium-high heat. Saute the cutlets until cooked through, about 3 minutes on each side. Transfer to a plate and cover to keep warm.

3 Add the pears, cranberries, and the brown sugar mixture to the skillet; bring to a boil. Simmer, uncovered, until the berries begin to pop and the chutney is thickened, about 5 minutes. Spoon the chutney over the cutlets.

What's for Dinner

 Complete the menu with oven-roasted Brussels sprouts and fresh quick-cooking pasta, such as fettuccini.

 COOK'S TIP To roast Brussels sprouts, coat the sprouts with a bit of olive oil and roast them on a baking sheet in a preheated 450°F oven until browned, about 20 minutes. Shake the pan a few times so that the sprouts brown evenly.

Per serving:

5 POINTS per serving   260 Calories • 3 g Total Fat • 1 g Saturated Fat • 66 mg Cholesterol • 402 mg Sodium • 30 mg Total Carbohydrate
2 g Dietary Fiber • 27 g Protein • 42 mg Calcium

Pepper-Crusted Flank Steak with Cucumber Relish

The cool and refreshing cucumber relish balances the heat of the spicy, peppery steak. For a flavorful taste twist, add a few crushed fennel or cumin seeds to the cracked black pepper.

*Makes 4 servings
(yields 2 cups relish)*

3 tablespoons molasses

2 teaspoons cracked black pepper

1/2 teaspoon salt

1 (1-pound) flank steak, trimmed of all visible fat

1 large cucumber, peeled, seeded, and chopped (about 1 1/2 cups)

1 small carrot, diced

2 large scallions, finely chopped

2 tablespoons sugar

1 tablespoon rice vinegar

1 tablespoon reduced-sodium soy sauce

1 Preheat the broiler. Coat the rack of a broiler pan with nonstick spray.

2 Combine the molasses, pepper, and salt in a small bowl. Rub the mixture over both sides of the steak. Broil the steak 4 inches from the heat until done to taste, about 6 minutes on each side for medium-rare. Remove from the broiler, cover loosely with foil, and let stand 5 minutes before slicing.

3 Meanwhile, combine the cucumber, carrot, scallions, sugar, vinegar, and soy sauce in a bowl; serve the relish on the side.

What's for Dinner

 Couscous, the flavorful Moroccan pasta, makes a speedy side dish to the steak; choose a plain, quick-cooking couscous or one of the flavored varieties, such as sun-dried tomato.

6 *POINTS* per serving

Per serving:
279 Calories • 9 g Total Fat • 4 g Saturated Fat • 46 mg Cholesterol • 497 mg Sodium • 21 mg Total Carbohydrate
1 g Dietary Fiber • 28 g Protein • 57 mg Calcium

Pepper-Crusted Flank Steak with Cucumber Relish

Oriental Pepper Steak

Lean flank steak is the main attraction in this ever-popular stir-fry. Be sure to slice the meat very thinly—this speeds up cooking time and makes the beef more tender.

Makes 6 servings

2 teaspoons canola oil

1 pound flank steak, cut against the grain into thin strips

1 red bell pepper, seeded and cut into $1/4$-inch strips

1 green bell pepper, seeded and cut into $1/4$-inch strips

1 onion, cut into $1/4$-inch-thick slices

2 tablespoons reduced-sodium soy sauce

1 $1/2$ tablespoons cornstarch

1 $3/4$ cups beef broth

 Heat the oil in a large nonstick skillet until nearly smoking. Add the steak and stir-fry until lightly browned, about 4 minutes. Transfer to a bowl.

2 Add the bell peppers and onion to the skillet. Cover and cook over medium heat until the vegetables are softened, about 6 minutes. Remove the cover and continue cooking until the vegetables are tender and browned, about 4 minutes longer.

3 Meanwhile, whisk together the soy sauce and cornstarch in a bowl; whisk in the beef broth. Return the steak to the skillet, along with the soy sauce mixture. Cook until the sauce boils and thickens, about 3 minutes.

What's for Dinner

 Serve this stir-fry over your favorite rice, of course!

COOK'S TIP For easier pre-stir-fry slicing, pop the steak into the freezer for 30 minutes. Then, slice the beef thinly; hold a sharp knife almost parallel to the work surface and cut the meat on an angle, across the grain, into paper-thin slices.

4 POINTS per serving

Per serving:
189 Calories • 10 g Total Fat • 4 g Saturated Fat • 39 mg Cholesterol • 475 mg Sodium • 8 mg Total Carbohydrate
1 g Dietary Fiber • 17 g Protein • 13 mg Calcium

Pork Chops with Sweet Corn Relish

A comfortingly old-fashioned filling meal, this is reminiscent of a Midwestern Sunday supper, right down to a sweet corn relish that could easily win a best-of-fair prize. By all means use fresh sweet corn during those months when it is plentiful.

Makes 4 servings
(yield 2 cups relish)

2 cups fresh or thawed frozen corn kernels

1/4 cup seeded and chopped green bell pepper

1/4 cup seeded and chopped red bell pepper

1/4 cup chopped red onion

2 tablespoons sugar

2 tablespoon cider vinegar

1/4 teaspoon ground cinnamon

1/8 teaspoon ground ginger

3/4 teaspoon salt

1/4 teaspoon coarsely ground black pepper

4 (4-ounce) boneless thin-cut pork loin chops, trimmed of all visible fat

2 teaspoon canola oil

1 Combine the corn, bell peppers, onion, sugar, vinegar, cinnamon, ginger, 1/2 teaspoon of the salt, and 1/8 teaspoon of the black pepper in a saucepan. Cook over medium heat, stirring occasionally, until heated through, about 5 minutes; remove from the heat.

2 Sprinkle the pork chops with the remaining 1/4 teaspoon salt and 1/8 teaspoon black pepper. Heat the oil in a large nonstick skillet over medium-high heat. Add the chops and cook until browned and cooked through, about 3 minutes on each side.

What's for Dinner

Serve this dish family-style with baked apple wedges.

 COOK'S TIP If you use frozen corn, be sure to drain any excess liquid after the kernels have thawed.

6 POINTS per serving

Per serving:
307 Calories • 10 g Total Fat • 3 g Saturated Fat • 70 mg Cholesterol • 687 mg Sodium • 29 mg Total Carbohydrate • 3 g Dietary Fiber • 29 g Protein • 34 mg Calcium

Garlic Pork Chops with Texmati Rice

These robust chops are best paired with the fragrant basmati rice of India, or with Texmati rice, the milder American variety. Cooking times for these rices can vary greatly so read package cooking directions carefully. If you can't find a brand that will cook in 15 to 20 minutes, substitute a quick-cooking rice of your choice.

Makes 4 servings

1 cup Texmati or basmati rice

2 tablespoons all-purpose flour

2 teaspoons paprika

1 teaspoon garlic powder

1 teaspoon ground coriander

1/4 teaspoon salt

1/8 teaspoon coarsely ground black pepper

4 (4-ounce) boneless center-cut pork loin chops, trimmed of all visible fat

2 tablespoons butter

3 garlic cloves, minced

1/2 cup fat-free, reduced-sodium chicken broth

1 tablespoon red wine vinegar

1 Cook the rice according to package directions.

2 Meanwhile, combine the flour, paprika, garlic powder, coriander, salt, and pepper in a bowl; coat both sides of the pork chops with the mixture.

3 Melt the butter in a large nonstick skillet over medium–high heat. Add the chops and cook 4 minutes. Turn the chops over and cook until browned and cooked through, about 3 minutes longer; transfer to a plate. To the skillet, add the garlic, broth, and vinegar; bring to a boil and cook 3–4 minutes (the volume of liquid in the pan will be reduced to between 1/4 cup and 1/3 cup). Return the chops to the pan and cook 2 minutes, turning once, to heat through. Serve with the rice.

What's for Dinner

 All you need to round out this generous meal is a steamed green, such as kale, Swiss chard, mustard greens, or baby spinach.

 COOK'S TIP You can find bags of washed baby spinach in the produce section with quick microwave-in-the-bag directions.

10 *POINTS* per serving

Per serving:
431 Calories • 14 g Total Fat • 6 g Saturated Fat • 79 mg Cholesterol • 329 mg Sodium • 43 mg Total Carbohydrate
1 g Dietary Fiber • 29 g Protein • 37 mg Calcium

Peachy Pork Chops

Like game, many cuts of pork are complemented by a fruit sauce or glaze. When preparing these chops, you could easily substitute apricot preserves or orange marmalade for the peach preserves—with equally delicious results.

Makes 4 servings

¹/₂ cup peach preserves

1 garlic clove, finely minced

2 tablespoons Dijon mustard

1 tablespoon reduced-sodium soy sauce

2 tablespoons orange juice

¹/₄ teaspoon crushed red pepper

4 (5-ounce) thin-cut bone-in pork loin chops

¹/₂ teaspoon salt

¹/₄ teaspoon coarsely ground black pepper

1 teaspoon canola oil

 Combine the peach preserves, garlic, mustard, soy sauce, orange juice, and crushed red pepper in a small bowl.

2 Sprinkle the chops with the salt and black pepper. Heat the oil in a large nonstick skillet over medium–high heat. Saute the pork chops until browned and cooked through, 4–5 minutes on each side; transfer to a plate and cover to keep warm. Add the peach mixture to the skillet; bring to a boil. Reduce the heat and simmer, uncovered, until the sauce thickens slightly, about 3 minutes. Spoon the sauce over the chops.

What's for Dinner

These flavorful chops go well with quick-cooking brown rice or mild Israeli couscous.

 COOK'S TIP To save even more time, look for instant brown rice in your supermarket—it only needs to be reconstituted, much the same way as quick-cooking couscous.

6 *POINTS* per serving

Per serving:
264 Calories • 6 g Total Fat • 2 g Saturated Fat • 56 mg Cholesterol • 541 mg Sodium • 30 mg Total Carbohydrate
1 g Dietary Fiber • 21 g Protein • 40 mg Calcium

Pork Schnitzel with Escarole Salad

The traditional wiener schnitzel *is a fried veal cutlet, but to cut down on fat, we broil lean (and economical!) pork cutlets. For a new rendition of this favorite dish, we set our healthy version on a bed of leafy greens.*

Makes 4 servings

2 tablespoons cider vinegar

1 tablespoon olive oil

1 teaspoon Dijon mustard

3/4 teaspoon salt

1/2 teaspoon coarsely ground black pepper

1/2 head escarole, cleaned and chopped (about 6 cups)

1 Vidalia onion, thinly sliced

3/4 cup seasoned dried bread crumbs

1 pound boneless pork loin cutlets

3 tablespoons reduced-calorie mayonnaise

1 Preheat the broiler.

2 Whisk together the vinegar, oil, mustard, 1/4 teaspoon of the salt, and 1/4 teaspoon of the pepper in a large bowl. Add the escarole and onion and toss to mix.

3 Put the bread crumbs into a shallow bowl. Sprinkle the cutlets with the remaining 1/2 teaspoon salt and 1/4 teaspoon pepper. Brush both sides of each cutlet with mayonnaise, then dip to coat in the bread crumbs. Place the cutlets on the rack of a broiler pan; spray the cutlets lightly with nonstick spray. Broil 4 inches from the heat until browned, about 3 minutes on each side.

4 Divide the escarole mixture among 4 plates; top each with a cutlet.

What's for Dinner

 Instead of the typically heavy spaetzle accompaniment, serve this dish with yolkless egg noodles.

 COOK'S TIP In addition to buying the precut variety, you can also fashion pork cutlets at home by cutting 1/4-inch-thick rounds from a small pork tenderloin and pounding them thin between two sheets of plastic wrap.

8 POINTS per serving

Per serving:
354 Calories • 15 g Total Fat • 4 g Saturated Fat • 74 mg Cholesterol • 1,176 mg Sodium • 24 mg Total Carbohydrate • 4 g Dietary Fiber • 30 g Protein • 98 mg Calcium

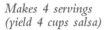

Ham Steak with Fruit Salsa

A succulent fruit salsa nicely counters the saltiness of the ham steak. The salsa is very versatile; you can substitute lemon juice for the lime juice, mint for the cilantro, or any seasonal fruit for the peaches and plums.

*Makes 4 servings
(yield 4 cups salsa)*

2 peaches, diced

6 plums, diced

1/4 cup finely chopped red onion

1/2 jalapeño pepper, seeded and finely chopped (wear gloves to prevent irritation)

2 tablespoons fresh lime juice

2 tablespoons chopped cilantro

1 tablespoon Dijon mustard

1 tablespoon packed dark brown sugar

1 (1-pound) ham steak

 1 Preheat the broiler.

2 Combine the peaches, plums, onion, jalapeño pepper, lime juice, and cilantro in a bowl.

3 Combine the mustard and sugar in a small bowl. Place the ham steak on the rack of a broiler pan and broil, 4 inches from the heat, 4 minutes. Turn the ham over and brush with the mustard mixture; broil 4 minutes longer. Cut the steak into 4 portions and top each with 1 cup of the fruit salsa.

What's for Dinner

Give this dish a Southern accent and serve with hominy, the dried corn from which the Southern staple grits are ground. It comes precooked in cans, so just warm it in a skillet before serving.

4 POINTS per serving

Per serving:
218 Calories • 5 g Total Fat • 1 g Saturated Fat • 60 mg Cholesterol • 1,515 mg Sodium • 24 mg Total Carbohydrate • 3 g Dietary Fiber • 21 g Protein • 18 mg Calcium

Tortellini with Prosciutto and Peas in a Creamy Sauce

Deliciously wonderful pastas such as tortellini, ("little cakes" in Italian), can be found in the refrigerator cases of most supermarkets. For this comforting dish we use cheese-stuffed tortellini and add prosciutto, a seasoned and salt-cured Italian ham, to the creamy sauce.

Makes 4 servings (yield 8 cups)

$1/2$ pound refrigerated fresh cheese tortellini

1 cup frozen peas

$1/4$ pound deli-sliced prosciutto, chopped

2 tablespoons all-purpose flour

1 cup whole milk

$1/2$ cup grated Parmesan cheese

$1/2$ teaspoon coarsely ground black pepper

 Bring a large pot of water to a boil. Add the tortellini and cook according to package directions. Stir in the peas during the last 2 minutes of cooking; drain.

 Meanwhile, coat a large nonstick skillet with nonstick spray and heat over medium heat. Add the prosciutto and cook, stirring occasionally, until lightly browned, 2–3 minutes. Remove and reserve the prosciutto. Dissolve the flour in the milk in a small bowl and add to the skillet. Cook, stirring constantly, until thickened, 8–10 minutes. Remove from the heat and stir in the Parmesan cheese and pepper. Add the prosciutto, tortellini, and peas and toss to coat.

What's for Dinner

Begin the meal with a warm asparagus or spinach salad.

COOK'S TIP Although the exquisite *Prosciutto di Parma* is usually the first choice in prosciuttos, when eaten uncooked, the less expensive domestic prosciutto is fine in a cooked sauce such as this.

6 POINTS per serving

Per serving:
358 Calories • 0 g Total Fat • 6 g Saturated Fat • 66 mg Cholesterol • 1,236 mg Sodium • 38 mg Total Carbohydrate
4 g Dietary Fiber • 25 g Protein • 324 mg Calcium

Tortellini with Prosciutto and Peas in a Creamy Sauce

minute recipes

DINNER

Maple-Berry Pancakes

These pancakes are topped not just with syrup, but with a refreshing and healthy berry and kiwi mixture, flavored with maple syrup and fragrant fresh mint. Try the topping on angel food cake, pound cake, or mixed into your favorite yogurt.

*Makes 4 servings
(yield 12 pancakes and
4 cups topping)*

2 cups strawberries,
hulled and sliced

1 cup raspberries

1 cup blueberries

1 kiwi, peeled and finely
chopped

3 tablespoons chopped
fresh mint

1/2 cup light maple
pancake syrup

2 cups reduced-fat
all-purpose baking mix

1 1/4 cups low-fat
(1%) milk

1 large egg, lightly beaten

3/4 teaspoon ground
cinnamon

 Combine the strawberries, raspberries, blueberries, kiwi, mint, and 1/4 cup of the syrup in a bowl.

 In another bowl, whisk together the baking mix, milk, egg, cinnamon, and the remaining 1/4 cup syrup.

3 Spray a nonstick griddle or large skillet with nonstick spray. Using 1/4 cup for each pancake, pour the batter onto the pan. Cook just until the tops are covered with bubbles and the edges look cooked, 2–3 minutes. Flip and cook until browned, about 2 minutes longer. Top the pancakes with the berry mixture and serve.

What's for Breakfast

 Serve grilled slices of Canadian bacon on the side.

7 POINTS per serving

Per serving (3 pancakes with 1 cup topping):
366 Calories • 7 g Total Fat • 2 g Saturated Fat • 56 mg Cholesterol • 772 mg Sodium • 68 mg Total Carbohydrate
6 g Dietary Fiber • 10 g Protein • 198 mg Calcium

Maple-Berry Pancakes

Banana-Chocolate Chip Pancakes

*Makes 4 servings
(yield 12 pancakes)*

1½ cups all-purpose flour

1 tablespoon sugar

2 teaspoons baking powder

¼ teaspoon salt

⅛ teaspoon ground ginger

2 ripe bananas, mashed

1 cup fat-free milk

1 large egg, lightly beaten

1 teaspoon vanilla extract

¼ cup mini chocolate chips

The French have crêpes, the Russians blinis, and we have our breakfast favorite, the pancake. Kids especially will love this banana and chocolate combination. Top the pancakes with maple syrup or with a simple sprinkle of powdered sugar.

1 Combine the flour, sugar, baking powder, salt, and ginger in a bowl. In a separate bowl, combine the bananas, milk, egg, and vanilla. Stir the flour mixture into the banana mixture until smooth. Gently fold in the mini chocolate chips. Let the batter stand at room temperature for 10–15 minutes.

2 Preheat a nonstick griddle or large nonstick skillet over medium heat. Using a scant ¼ cup for each pancake, pour the batter onto the pan. Cook just until the tops are covered with bubbles and the edges are browned, 2–3 minutes. Flip and cook until browned, about 2 minutes longer. Serve immediately.

What's for Breakfast

Serve the pancakes with crisp-cooked turkey bacon or lean sausage and applesauce.

COOK'S TIP For an easy breakfast anytime you want it, make a batch of the pancakes ahead of time. Let them cool to room temperature, then wrap single portions in heavy-duty plastic wrap and freeze until ready to use. Simply microwave the pancakes on High for one to two minutes to heat through.

6 POINTS per serving

Per serving (3 pancakes):
334 Calories • 5 g Total Fat • 3 g Saturated Fat • 54 mg Cholesterol • 393 mg Sodium • 63 mg Total Carbohydrate • 3 g Dietary Fiber • 10 g Protein • 131 mg Calcium

Southwestern Strata

Baked in custard cups, these individual layered casseroles are perfect for breakfast, brunch, or a light lunch. The mild green chiles and modest dose of hot pepper sauce add a light touch of spice with a Southwestern accent. By all means, if you like your food spicy, add more sauce.

Makes 4 servings

4 slices white bread, cut into 1-inch cubes

¹/4 pound fat-free deli ham, chopped

¹/4 pound light Jarlsberg cheese, shredded

2 large eggs

2 egg whites

1¹/2 cups low-fat (1%) milk

2 teaspoons canned chopped mild green chiles, drained

4 drops hot pepper sauce

1 Preheat the oven to 400°F. Spray four 10-ounce custard cups with nonstick spray.

2 Line the bottoms of the custard cups with the bread cubes. Top each with the ham and cheese.

3 Whisk together the eggs, egg whites, milk, chiles, and pepper sauce in a bowl. Divide the mixture evenly among the custard cups. Place the cups on a baking pan and bake until puffed and golden, and a knife inserted in the center comes out clean, about 25 minutes.

What's for Breakfast

 Serve with a fresh fruit assortment and mini muffins.

 COOK'S TIP For a lazy-morning breakfast, assemble the stratas in the custard cups the night before; cover and refrigerate them. The next morning, simply uncover them and bake as directed above.

Per serving:
255 Calories • 9 g Total Fat • 4 g Saturated Fat • 134 mg Cholesterol • 615 mg Sodium • 18 mg Total Carbohydrate
1 g Dietary Fiber • 23 g Protein • 460 mg Calcium

6 POINTS per serving

Potato Leek Soup

Warming and wonderful on a wintry day, this simple soup also makes a great hot weather dish when served chilled. For the classic cold version, known as vichyssoise, just refrigerate the soup until well chilled, then garnish with snipped chives.

Makes 6 servings (yield 7 cups)

1 1/2 pounds baking potatoes, peeled and chopped

2 leeks, pale green and white parts only, cleaned and chopped

4 cups fat-free, reduced-sodium chicken broth

1/2 teaspoon dried thyme

3/4 cup half-and-half

1/2 teaspoon salt

1/4 teaspoon coarsely ground black pepper

1 Combine the potatoes, leeks, broth, and thyme in a large saucepan. Cover and bring to a boil over high heat. Reduce the heat and simmer until the potatoes are tender, about 20 minutes.

2 Puree the soup in a food processor or blender, in batches if necessary. Return the soup to the pan, stir in the half-and-half, salt, and pepper, and cook for 1 minute longer to heat through.

What's for Lunch

 Hot or cold, the soup is excellent with a crusty French baguette followed by fresh seasonal fruit.

3 POINTS per serving

Per serving (1 generous cup):
157 Calories • 4 g Total Fat • 2 g Saturated Fat • 11 mg Cholesterol • 587 mg Sodium • 27 mg Total Carbohydrate
2 g Dietary Fiber • 5 g Protein • 72 mg Calcium

Italian Bean Soup

This classic bean and potato soup features cannellini, or white kidney beans, as well as the more familiar red kidney and fresh green beans. Be sure to rinse and drain the canned beans thoroughly before cooking, which will improve the flavor, as well as rid the beans of any residual salt.

*Makes 6 servings
(yield 10 cups)*

1 teaspoon olive oil

1 onion, finely chopped

2 garlic cloves, minced

2 plum tomatoes, chopped

4 cups reduced-sodium chicken broth

2 medium baking potatoes, peeled and cubed

2 zucchini (3/4 pound), cut into 1-inch chunks

1/2 pound green beans, cut into 2-inch pieces

1 (15-ounce) can red kidney beans, rinsed and drained

1 (15-ounce) can cannellini beans, rinsed and drained

3 tablespoons grated Parmesan cheese

Heat the oil in a nonstick saucepan over medium-low heat. Add the onion and garlic; cook until the onion is very tender, about 8 minutes. Stir in the tomatoes and continue to cook until they are very soft, about 5 minutes. Add the broth and potatoes; bring to a boil. Cover and simmer until the potatoes are almost tender, about 10 minutes. Stir in the zucchini, green beans, kidney beans, and cannellini beans. Re-cover and cook until the vegetables are tender, about 8 minutes longer. Stir in the Parmesan cheese.

What's for Lunch

Serve with an assortment of crostini, little Italian open-faced sandwiches, made by topping slices of toasted Italian bread with cheese, bean spread, pâté, roasted sweet red peppers, or baby shrimp.

4 POINTS per serving

Per serving (generous 1 1/2 cup):
226 Calories • 2 g Total Fat • 1 g Saturated Fat • 2 mg Cholesterol • 771 mg Sodium • 40 mg Total Carbohydrate
12 g Dietary Fiber • 13 g Protein • 116 mg Calcium

Mediterranean Hero

Brimming with eggplant rounds, roasted peppers, tomatoes, mozzarella cheese, and fresh basil, this sandwich is a veritable garden in a roll. You can substitute other favorite grilled or broiled vegetables such as zucchini, onions, or carrots.

Makes 4 servings

1 (1^{1}/4-pound) eggplant, cut into ^{1}/4-inch rounds

3 tablespoons balsamic vinegar

1 tablespoon extra-virgin olive oil

1 teaspoon Dijon mustard

8 slices Italian bread, toasted

2 large tomatoes, cut into ^{1}/4-inch slices

^{1}/2 pound package part-skim mozzarella cheese, cut into ^{1}/4-inch slices

1 (12-ounce) jar roasted sweet red peppers, drained

1 cup loosely packed basil leaves

 Preheat the broiler. Spray the rack of a broiler pan with nonstick spray. Arrange the eggplant rounds on the rack and spray lightly with non-stick spray. Broil, 5 inches from the heat, until golden and tender, about 8 minutes, turning once.

 Whisk together the vinegar, oil, and mustard in a small bowl. Brush 4 slices of the toast with the vinaigrette, then layer each with the egg-plant, tomatoes, mozzarella cheese, roasted peppers, and basil. Cover with the remaining slices of toast. Cut each sandwich in half on the diagonal.

What's for Lunch

Serve with a crisp iceberg lettuce salad for a complete meal.

9 *POINTS* per serving

Per serving:
410 Calories • 15 g Total Fat • 7 g Saturated Fat • 32 mg Cholesterol • 750 mg Sodium • 48 mg Total Carbohydrate
6 g Dietary Fiber • 21 g Protein • 436 mg Calcium

Lentil and Spinach Salad with Curry Vinaigrette

The dressing is what makes this spinach salad truly unforgettable. A zingy vinaigrette made with toasted curry powder, it's sure to invigorate your taste buds.

Makes 4 servings
(yield 8 cups)

1 cup lentils, rinsed and picked over

$1/2$ cup chopped onion

4 cups water

2 tablespoons red wine vinegar

1 tablespoon extra-virgin olive oil

1 tablespoon curry powder, toasted

$1/2$ teaspoon salt

4 cups loosely packed baby spinach, cleaned and coarsely chopped

1 (15-ounce) can garbanzo beans, rinsed and drained

1 cup cherry tomatoes, halved

1 green bell pepper, seeded and finely chopped

1 cup peeled, seeded, and finely chopped cucumber

 1 Combine the lentils, onion, and water in a saucepan; bring to a boil. Cover, reduce the heat, and simmer until the lentils are tender, about 20 minutes; drain.

2 Meanwhile, whisk together the vinegar, oil, curry powder, and salt in a large bowl. Add the lentils, spinach, garbanzo beans, tomatoes, bell pepper, and cucumber; toss to coat.

What's for Lunch

 Serve with crispy hash-brown potatoes on the side.

COOK'S TIP Toasting spices eliminates their raw edge and intensifies flavor. Toast in a small dry skillet over low heat, shaking the pan often, just until the spice becomes fragrant. The heat level of this dish will vary according to the grade of curry powder you use, from mild to madras (hot).

6 POINTS per serving

Per serving:
323 Calories • 6 g Total Fat • 1 g Saturated Fat • 0 mg Cholesterol • 532 mg Sodium • 50 mg Total Carbohydrate
24 g Dietary Fiber • 21 g Protein • 104 mg Calcium

Quinoa Salad with Fruit and Nuts

Makes 4 servings
(yield 5 cups)

2 cups water

1 cup quinoa, rinsed well under warm running water and drained

$^{1}/_{2}$ cup pitted chopped dates

$^{1}/_{2}$ cup mixed dried fruit, chopped

3 scallions, chopped

3 tablespoons chopped cilantro

3 tablespoons pine nuts, toasted

2 tablespoons fresh lime juice

1 tablespoon olive oil

2 teaspoons honey

$^{1}/_{2}$ teaspoon salt

Popular in South American kitchens, quinoa is cooked much like rice. Before preparing quinoa, you must first rinse the grain under warm running water to wash away the saporins, a natural substance that deters birds and wildlife from eating the grain and lends a bitter-tasting edge if not washed off.

 Bring the water to a boil in a saucepan. Add the quinoa, cover, and cook, until tender and the water has evaporated, about 15 minutes. Transfer to a large bowl and stir in the dates, mixed fruit, scallions, cilantro, and pine nuts.

 Whisk together the lime juice, oil, honey, and salt in a small bowl. Pour the dressing over the quinoa mixture and toss to coat.

What's for Lunch

Finish with a medley of sliced melons.

7 POINTS per serving

Per serving:
353 Calories • 9 g Total Fat • 1 g Saturated Fat • 0 mg Cholesterol • 306 mg Sodium • 64 mg Total Carbohydrate
6 g Dietary Fiber • 8 g Protein • 54 mg Calcium

Asian Noodle Salad

Although this salad starts with Italian vermicelli rather than Asian noodles, it has a distinctly Asian flavor—thanks to the sesame oil, soy sauce, and rice vinegar. It's colorfully dotted with red, green, and yellow bell peppers, as well as carrots, and boasts toasted sesame seeds and fresh ginger. If you like, substitute rice or soba noodles for an authentic Asian touch.

*Makes 4 servings
(yield 6 cups)*

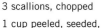

1/2 pound vermicelli

1 red bell pepper, seeded and thinly sliced

1 green bell pepper, seeded and thinly sliced

1 yellow bell pepper, seeded and thinly sliced

1 cup shredded carrots

3 scallions, chopped

1 cup peeled, seeded, and diced cucumber

1/2 cup chopped cilantro

1/4 cup seasoned rice vinegar

1 tablespoon Asian (dark) sesame oil

1 tablespoon reduced-sodium soy sauce

1 tablespoon sesame seeds, toasted

1 teaspoon sugar

1/2 teaspoon grated peeled fresh ginger

 Bring a large pot of water to a boil. Add the vermicelli and cook according to package directions; drain. Transfer to a large bowl and add the bell peppers, carrots, scallions, cucumber, and cilantro.

 Whisk together the vinegar, oil, soy sauce, sesame seeds, sugar, and ginger in a small bowl. Pour the dressing over the pasta and vegetables; toss to coat.

What's for Lunch

Serve an assortment of rice crackers with the salad.

 To toast sesame seeds, heat in a small dry skillet over low heat, shaking the skillet occasionally, until the seeds begin to turn golden brown, about five minutes.

6 POINTS per serving

Per serving:
338 Calories • 6 g Total Fat • 1 g Saturated Fat • 0 mg Cholesterol • 624 mg Sodium • 62 mg Total Carbohydrate
5 g Dietary Fiber • 10 g Protein • 70 mg Calcium

LUNCH

Layered Vegetable Terrine

This no-bake terrine makes an impressive lunch or first course. It's chock-full of fresh eggplant and squash and finished with aromatic fresh basil, sweet balsamic vinegar, and pungent goat cheese.

Makes 4 servings
(yield 2/3 cup sauce)

1 (1½-pound) eggplant, cut lengthwise into ¼-inch slices

1 (½-pound) zucchini, cut lengthwise into ¼-inch slices

1 (½-pound) yellow squash, cut lengthwise into ¼-inch slices

1 (12-ounce) jar roasted sweet red peppers, drained

3 tablespoons chopped fresh basil + 1 cup loosely packed basil leaves

2 tablespoons balsamic vinegar

2 tablespoons water

1 tablespoon extra-virgin olive oil

¼ teaspoon salt

2 ounces goat cheese, cut into small pieces

1 Preheat the broiler. Spray two baking pans with nonstick spray.

2 Place the eggplant, zucchini, and yellow squash in a single layer on the baking pans; lightly spray with nonstick spray. Broil the vegetables, 5 inches from the heat, until tender and golden, about 15 minutes.

3 Reserving 1 cup of the roasted peppers, combine the remaining peppers with the chopped basil, vinegar, water, oil, and salt in a food processor or blender and puree.

4 Arrange the eggplant crosswise in an 8 × 4-inch loaf pan so that a bit drapes over each side of the pan. Layer the zucchini, yellow squash, the remaining roasted peppers, goat cheese, and basil leaves over the eggplant in the pan. Fold the draping eggplant ends over the top and press down. Invert the loaf pan onto an oval plate and slowly remove the pan, dislodging the terrine. Cut the terrine crosswise into eight 1-inch slices and serve with the roasted red pepper sauce.

What's for Lunch

 Serve along with an arugula or watercress salad and a crusty French baguette.

 COOK'S TIP Depending upon the size of your broiler, you may need to broil the vegetables, one baking sheet at a time. Or roast the vegetables in a 500°F oven 15–20 minutes, until tender and browned.

3 POINTS per serving

Per serving:
146 Calories • 7 g Total Fat • 3 g Saturated Fat • 7 mg Cholesterol • 332 mg Sodium • 17 mg Total Carbohydrate • 6 g Dietary Fiber • 6 g Protein • 66 mg Calcium

Potato, Onion, and Rosemary Frittata

Frittatas can be finished either in a high-heat oven or under a broiler. Our tasty version is broiled and the result is delicious! In addition to lunch, this dish works well for brunch or as a light supper.

Makes 4 servings

1 large baking potato, peeled and cubed

2 teaspoons olive oil

1 large onion, thinly sliced

2 teaspoons chopped fresh rosemary

3 large eggs

4 egg whites

$^1/_2$ teaspoon salt

$^1/_4$ teaspoon coarsely ground black pepper

1 tablespoon water

 Preheat the broiler.

 Cook the potato in a pot of boiling water until tender, about 10 minutes; drain.

3 Heat the oil in a nonstick skillet over medium-low heat. Add the onion and cook until golden and tender, about 10 minutes. Add the potato and rosemary. Cook, stirring occasionally about 5 minutes longer to blend flavors.

4 Meanwhile, whisk together the eggs, egg whites, salt, pepper, and water; pour over the onion and potato mixture in the skillet. Cook, lifting the edges of the frittata with a rubber spatula so that uncooked egg can run underneath, until almost set, about 4 minutes.

5 Transfer the skillet to the broiler and broil, 5 inches from the heat, until the top is set and the frittata is cooked through, about 2 minutes. Invert the frittata onto a plate and cut into wedges before serving.

What's for Lunch

 Pair with steaming mugs of French onion soup.

COOK'S TIP Be sure to use a nonstick skillet with curved sides. This will allow the frittata to slip out easily from the pan. If your skillet does not have an ovenproof handle, wrap it in heavy-duty foil before putting it under the broiler.

3 *POINTS* per serving

Per serving:
153 Calories • 6 g Total Fat • 2 g Saturated Fat • 159 mg Cholesterol • 396 mg Sodium • 15 mg Total Carbohydrate
2 g Dietary Fiber • 10 g Protein • 32 mg Calcium

Asparagus and Potato Frittata

Frittatas, a great addition to a lunch or brunch buffet, are flat, open-faced, Italian omelets in which the filling is mixed with the eggs, rather than folded inside the omelet. In Italy, frittatas are usually served at room temperature. You can also cut a frittata into wedges and serve it as a tasty sandwich filling.

Makes 4 servings

1 large baking potato, peeled and thinly sliced

1 pound asparagus, trimmed and cut into 1/2-inch pieces

4 large eggs

4 egg whites

1/2 cup fat-free milk

1/2 teaspoon salt

1/4 teaspoon baking powder

1/4 cup grated Parmesan cheese

1 onion, chopped

1 Preheat the oven to 500°F.

2 Put the potato into a saucepan and add sufficient water to cover by 3 inches. Cover the saucepan and bring to a boil over high heat; boil 5 minutes. Add the asparagus and cook 2 minutes longer. Drain and set aside to cool.

3 Combine the whole eggs, egg whites, milk, salt, baking powder, and 3 tablespoons of the Parmesan cheese in a bowl. Mix in the potato and asparagus.

4 Heat an ovenproof nonstick skillet over medium–high heat. Coat the skillet with nonstick spray and add the onion; cook, stirring occasionally, 2 minutes. Add the egg mixture and reduce the heat to medium. Cover and cook until almost set, about 10 minutes. Uncover the skillet, sprinkle with the remaining 1 tablespoon Parmesan cheese, and transfer to the oven. Bake until the frittata is cooked through and the cheese has browned, about 5 minutes. Invert the frittata onto a plate and cut into wedges before serving.

What's for Lunch

A simple Caesar salad would balance this meal perfectly.

166

4 POINTS per serving

Per serving:
199 Calories • 7 g Total Fat • 3 g Saturated Fat • 217 mg Cholesterol • 555 mg Sodium • 17 mg Total Carbohydrate
2 g Dietary Fiber • 16 g Protein • 155 mg Calcium

Asparagus and Potato Frittata

L U N C H

Peanut Noodles

This dish is as versatile as it is flavorful; the recipe works just as well with cooked chicken breast or pork tenderloin as with tofu. In addition to a satisfying lunch, the noodles can be served as a first course at dinner or a zesty accompaniment to a plain entrée.

Makes 4 servings (yield 6 cups)

1/2 pound spaghetti

2 carrots, sliced

1/4 pound snow peas

1 red bell pepper, seeded and thinly sliced

1/3 cup natural peanut butter

1/4 cup hoisin sauce

1 1/2 tablespoons packed dark brown sugar

1 1/2 tablespoons reduced-sodium soy sauce

1 tablespoon rice vinegar

1/2 teaspoon canola oil

1 tablespoon minced peeled fresh ginger

1 garlic clove, chopped

1/4 teaspoon crushed red pepper

1/2 pound low-fat firm tofu, cut into 1/4-inch cubes

2 tablespoons chopped unsalted peanuts

1 scallion, chopped

1 Bring a large pot of salted water to a boil. Add the spaghetti and cook according to package directions, adding the carrots, snow peas, and bell pepper during the last 2 minutes of cooking; reserve 1/2 cup pasta water and drain.

2 Combine the peanut butter, hoisin sauce, brown sugar, soy sauce, and vinegar in a bowl.

3 Heat the oil in a saucepan over medium-high heat. Add the ginger, garlic, and crushed red pepper; cook 30 seconds. Stir in the peanut butter mixture and the reserved pasta water. Cook 3 minutes, stir in the tofu, and continue to cook until hot, about 3 minutes longer. Toss in a large bowl with the pasta and vegetables, then transfer to a serving platter and sprinkle with the peanuts and scallion.

What's for Lunch

 The zesty noodles are best served with a cool and crisp slaw made with delicate Chinese cabbage.

 COOK'S TIP Toasted sesame seeds, sprinkled on at the last minute, add a lively nutty note to the noodles.

10 POINTS per serving

Per serving:
495 Calories • 15 g Total Fat • 2 g Saturated Fat • 0 mg Cholesterol • 696 mg Sodium • 70 mg Total Carbohydrate
6 g Dietary Fiber • 19 g Protein • 73 mg Calcium

Vermicelli with Vegetables

Lightly dressed and topped with the bounty of summer—tomato, thyme, zucchini, and basil—this is quick and refreshing luncheon party fare. Delicate thin-strand vermicelli pasta is best, although capellini would also work well.

*Makes 6 servings
(yield 12 cups)*

1 tablespoon olive oil

1 red onion, thinly sliced

2 garlic cloves, thinly sliced

1 tomato, chopped

1 tablespoon chopped
fresh thyme, or 1 teaspoon
dried

2 red potatoes, peeled and
cut into 1-inch cubes

2 zucchini (about
$^3/_4$ pound), cut into
1-inch cubes

4 cups reduced-sodium
chicken broth

$^1/_4$ pound vermicelli,
broken into 4-inch pieces

$^1/_2$ cup chopped fresh basil

3 tablespoons grated
Parmesan cheese

Heat the oil in a large nonstick saucepan over medium heat. Add the onion and garlic; cook until the onion begins to soften, about 5 minutes. Stir in the tomato and thyme; cook until both the tomato and onion are very tender, about 5 minutes longer. Add the potatoes, zucchini, and broth; bring to a boil. Cover and simmer until the vegetables are tender, about 10 minutes. Stir in the pasta and cook until tender, about 5 minutes longer. Remove from the heat and stir in basil and Parmesan cheese.

What's for Lunch

You'll need some crusty bread on the table for dunking in the pasta bowls.

3 POINTS per serving

Per serving:
174 Calories • 4 g Total Fat • 1 g Saturated Fat • 2 mg Cholesterol • 424 mg Sodium • 29 mg Total Carbohydrate
3 g Dietary Fiber • 8 g Protein • 76 mg Calcium

LUNCH

Red, Green, and Yellow Pepper Spaghetti Pie

Easily made ahead, and equally good warm or at room temperature, this colorful dish is perfect for a brunch buffet. For variety, try substituting sautéed mushrooms and caramelized onions for the bell pepper medley.

Makes 4 servings

¹/₂ pound spaghetti

¹/₃ cup seeded and chopped red bell pepper

¹/₃ cup seeded and chopped green bell pepper

¹/₃ cup seeded and chopped yellow bell pepper

¹/₃ cup chopped onion

¹/₄ cup grated Parmesan cheese

1 teaspoon dried basil

³/₄ teaspoon salt

¹/₄ teaspoon crushed red pepper

3 large eggs, lightly beaten

1 tablespoon olive oil

1 Bring a large pot of salted water to a boil. Cook the spaghetti according to package directions; drain.

2 Combine the bell peppers, onion, Parmesan cheese, basil, salt, and crushed red pepper in a large bowl. Add the spaghetti and eggs; tossing to coat.

3 Heat the oil in a nonstick skillet over medium heat. Add the spaghetti mixture, pressing down lightly with a spatula to form a cake, and cook until lightly golden on the bottom, about 4 minutes. Remove from the heat and invert a large plate over the skillet; flip to dislodge the spaghetti cake onto the plate, then slide the cake back into the skillet cooked-side up. Cook until golden on the second side, about 4 minutes longer. Cut into wedges before serving.

What's for Lunch

Perfect with a Caesar salad and sparkling Italian wine.

COOK'S TIP For the best results, use a ten-inch skillet, which in some cases measures eight inches across the bottom.

7 POINTS **per serving**

Per serving:
335 Calories • 10 g Total Fat • 3 g Saturated Fat • 163 mg Cholesterol • 654 mg Sodium • 47 mg Total Carbohydrate
2 g Dietary Fiber • 15 g Protein • 111 mg Calcium

Crab Cakes with Cilantro-Corn Salsa

We dip these crab cakes lightly in cornflake crumbs before sautéing, which lends extra crunch as well as flavor. They make a substantial lunch or a satisfying first course. The crabmeat is a bit of a splurge, but great taste is worth the price! Crab lovers on a budget might want to substitute an equal amount of surimi for the lump crabmeat.

Makes 4 servings

1 pound jumbo lump crabmeat, picked over

1/4 cup reduced-calorie mayonnaise

3 scallions, finely chopped

3 tablespoons plain dried bread crumbs

1 tablespoon coarse-grained Dijon mustard

2 teaspoons fresh lemon juice

1 teaspoon grated lemon zest

1 egg white

6 drops hot pepper sauce

1/2 cup cornflake crumbs

2 (10-ounce) packages frozen corn kernels, thawed

2 tomatoes, seeded and finely chopped

1/2 cup finely chopped red onion

1/4 cup chopped cilantro

1 jalapeño pepper, seeded and finely chopped (wear gloves to prevent irritation)

1 tablespoon cider vinegar

2 teaspoons extra-virgin olive oil

1/2 teaspoon salt

2 teaspoons canola oil

1 Combine the crabmeat, mayonnaise, scallions, bread crumbs, mustard, lemon juice, lemon zest, egg white, and pepper sauce in a bowl. Mix well and shape into 8 patties.

2 Sprinkle the cornflake crumbs onto a sheet of wax paper or a plate. Dip the cakes in the crumbs to coat; cover and refrigerate 15 minutes.

3 Combine the corn, tomatoes, red onion, cilantro, jalapeño pepper, vinegar, olive oil, and salt in a bowl.

4 Heat the canola oil in a large nonstick skillet over medium heat. Add the crab cakes and cook until crisp and golden, about 6 minutes, turning once and cooking in batches if necessary. Serve with the corn salsa.

What's for Lunch

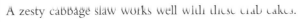 A zesty cabbage slaw works well with these crab cakes.

 COOK'S TIP Be sure to chill the crab cakes before cooking; this will help them set, so that they do not fall apart in the skillet.

Per serving:
402 Calories • 10 g Total Fat • 1 g Saturated Fat • 118 mg Cholesterol • 939 mg Sodium • 50 g Total Carbohydrate
5 g Dietary Fiber • 31 g Protein • 161 mg Calcium

8 POINTS per serving

LUNCH

Cornmeal Pancakes with Smoked Salmon and Caper Spread

This makes a spectacular dish for lunch or brunch. It can also be easily transformed into an hors d'oeuvre; just make quarter-size pancakes and top with smaller portions of smoked salmon and diminutive dollops of the caper spread. The pancakes are just as good at room temperature as they are hot, making them ideal for for entertaining.

Makes 4 servings (yield 12 pancakes)

$1/2$ cup nonfat sour cream

2 tablespoons finely chopped red onion

1 tablespoon capers, drained and chopped

1 teaspoon grated lemon zest

$1^1/2$ cups all-purpose flour

$1/2$ cup cornmeal

2 teaspoons baking powder

2 teaspoons sugar

1 teaspoon ground coriander

1 teaspoon salt

$1/4$ teaspoon cayenne

$1^1/3$ cups whole milk

1 large egg

$1/2$ pound sliced smoked salmon

1 Combine the sour cream, onion, capers, and lemon zest and set aside.

2 Combine the flour, cornmeal, baking powder, sugar, coriander, salt, and cayenne in a bowl. In another bowl, combine the milk and egg. Stir the flour mixture into the milk mixture until smooth. Let the batter stand at room temperature for 10–15 minutes.

3 Heat a nonstick griddle or large nonstick skillet over medium heat. Using a scant $1/4$ cup for each pancake, pour the batter onto the pan. Cook just until the tops are covered with bubbles and the edges look cooked, 2–3 minutes. Flip and cook until browned, about 2 minutes longer. Arrange 3 pancakes on each of 4 plates (do not stack). Top the servings with equal amounts of the smoked salmon and dollop each with 2 tablespoons of the sour cream mixture.

What's for Lunch

All you need to round out this meal is a tossed green salad and a pitcher of mimosas.

COOK'S TIP Allow time for the batter to rest before cooking. A few minutes are all that's needed to allow the proteins in the pancakes to "relax," yielding lighter fluffier pancakes.

8 POINTS per serving

Per serving:
405 Calories • 7 g Total Fat • 3 g Saturated Fat • 80 mg Cholesterol • 1,389 mg Sodium • 61 mg Total Carbohydrate
3 g Dietary Fiber • 22 g Protein • 195 mg Calcium

Vietnamese Chicken on Lettuce Leaves

*Makes 6 servings
(yield 6 cups)*

2 ounces rice noodles

1 tablespoon Asian (dark) sesame oil

2 teaspoons grated peeled fresh ginger

1 garlic clove, minced

1 pound ground skinless chicken breast

$1/2$ cup seeded and finely chopped red bell pepper

1 carrot, finely chopped

$1/3$ cup finely chopped cucumber

$1/3$ cup finely chopped red onion

6 tablespoons rice vinegar

$1/4$ cup honey

$1/4$ cup reduced-sodium soy sauce

$1/4$ cup chopped cilantro

3 tablespoons chopped unsalted peanuts

12 leaves Boston lettuce

This is elegant luncheon fare with a thoroughly up-to-date international accent. Redolent of ginger and cilantro and with just the right touch of sweetness from a hint of honey, the lunch is made pretty when served on leaves of Boston lettuce. The recipe is a snap to prepare; most of the preparation time is in the chopping, not the cooking, and can be done ahead of time if you like.

1 Bring a large pot of water to a boil. Cook the rice noodles according to package directions; rinse under cold running water, drain, and finely chop.

2 Heat 1 teaspoon of the oil in a large nonstick skillet. Add the ginger and garlic and cook, stirring, 30 seconds. Add the chicken and cook until cooked through and no longer pink, 6–7 minutes. Transfer to a large bowl and stir in the bell pepper, carrot, cucumber, onion, and noodles.

3 Combine the vinegar, honey, soy sauce, cilantro, peanuts, and the remaining 2 teaspoons oil in a small bowl. Add to the chicken mixture and toss well to combine. Arrange 2 lettuce leaves on each plate and mound the chicken on top.

What's for Lunch

A refreshing cucumber salad doused with wine vinegar pairs well with this dish.

COOK'S TIP Rice noodles, or cellophane noodles, are virtually free of fat and cholesterol. They can be found in the Asian section of most large supermarkets. They are great to serve as a side dish, dressed simply with a touch of sesame oil and soy sauce. The noodles are extremely fragile; take care not to overcook them.

Per serving:

7 POINTS **per serving**   303 Calories • 15 g Total Fat • 1 g Saturated Fat • 0 mg Cholesterol • 432 mg Sodium • 25 mg Total Carbohydrate
1 g Dietary Fiber • 16 g Protein • 37 mg Calcium

Crusty Chicken on Greens with Buttermilk Dressing

Makes 4 servings

3 tablespoons reduced-calorie mayonnaise

1 teaspoon fresh lemon juice

$3/4$ cup cornflake crumbs

4 (4-ounce) thin-sliced skinless boneless chicken breasts

$1/2$ cup buttermilk

$1/4$ cup light sour cream

1 tablespoon cider vinegar

1 teaspoon Worcerstershire sauce

1 teaspoon Dijon mustard

$1/2$ teaspoon salt

$1/2$ teaspoon sugar

8 cups baby greens

Heavy fried chicken will be a thing of the past when you try this delicious, crunchy cornflake coating. Served on a bed of baby greens with cool and crisp buttermilk dressing, it makes for an easy, yet indulgent, lunch.

1 Preheat the broiler. Spray the rack of a broiler pan with nonstick spray.

2 Combine the mayonnaise and lemon juice in a small bowl. Scatter the cornflake crumbs onto a sheet of wax paper. Brush the chicken breasts with the mayonnaise mixture, then press them into the crumbs to coat both sides. Arrange in a single layer on the baking rack and spray lightly with nonstick spray. Broil, 7 inches from the heat, until tender and golden, about 3 minutes on each side.

2 Whisk together the buttermilk, sour cream, vinegar, Worcestershire sauce, mustard, salt, and sugar in a small bowl. Arrange the salad greens on 4 plates. Cut each chicken breast on the diagonal into thirds. Top the greens on each plate with 3 pieces of chicken and drizzle with the dressing.

What's for Lunch

Pair with your favorite potato salad.

 COOK'S TIP To make a simple potato salad, toss cooked potato chunks with vinaigrette dressing, a little mayonnaise, and chopped fresh parsley.

Per serving:
259 Calories • 5 g Total Fat • 1 g Saturated Fat • 76 mg Cholesterol • 697 mg Sodium • 21 mg Total Carbohydrate
1 g Dietary Fiber • 31 g Protein • 123 mg Calcium

Smoked Chicken and New Potato Hash

Chicken hash, still found on the menus of famous eateries such as New York's 21 Club, is typically made with enough heavy cream and butter to cause any health-conscious diner to shudder. This version, boasting new potatoes and bell peppers, will please your taste buds without adding the extra fat and cholesterol. This is classic brunch fare, but it also makes a comforting supper.

Makes 4 servings (yield 4 cups)

1 tablespoon canola oil

1 pound new potatoes, thinly sliced

1 cup water

1 onion, chopped

1 red bell pepper, seeded and chopped

1 green bell pepper, seeded and chopped

2 teaspoons paprika

1/2 teaspoon fennel seeds

1/2 teaspoon garlic powder

3/4 teaspoon salt

1/4 teaspoon coarsely ground black pepper

3/4 pound skinless boneless chicken breasts, cut into thin strips

1 teaspoon liquid smoke

1 Heat 2 teaspoons of the oil in a large nonstick skillet over medium-high heat. Add the potatoes and cook 2 minutes. Add the water, onion, bell peppers, paprika, fennel seeds, garlic powder, 1/2 teaspoon of the salt, and the black pepper. Bring to a boil, cover, and cook, shaking the pan occasionally, 15 minutes. Uncover the skillet and continue to cook until the potatoes begin to brown slightly, about 5 minutes longer.

2 Meanwhile, toss the chicken in a bowl with the liquid smoke and sprinkle with the remaining 1/4 teaspoon salt. Heat the remaining 1 teaspoon oil in a nonstick skillet over medium-high heat. Add the chicken and cook, stirring occasionally, until cooked through, about 8 minutes. Stir the chicken into the hash and serve.

What's for Lunch

 Serve the hash with poached eggs and try it with the traditional garnish of chili sauce.

5 *POINTS* per serving

Per serving:
258 Calories • 5 g Total Fat • 1 g Saturated Fat • 49 mg Cholesterol • 500 mg Sodium • 31 mg Total Carbohydrate
4 g Dietary Fiber • 23 g Protein • 37 mg Calcium

Wagon Wheels with Turkey Chili

Called ruoti, *these wagon wheel-shaped morsels of pasta will delight the kids. To make a vegetarian dish, substitute one can of rinsed and drained red kidney beans for the turkey. Just add the beans with the tomatoes. Either way, finish with a sprinkle of reduced-fat cheddar cheese.*

*Makes 6 servings
(yield 6 cups)*

1 tablespoon canola oil

2 garlic cloves, minced

1 onion, chopped

1 green bell pepper, seeded and chopped

1 pound lean ground skinless turkey

1 (28-ounce) can whole peeled tomatoes, drained and chopped

2 tablespoons tomato paste

1 tablespoon chili powder

2 teaspoons ground cumin

1 teaspoon dried oregano

3/4 teaspoon salt

1/4 teaspoon cayenne

3/4 pound wagon wheel pasta

1 Heat the oil in a large nonstick skillet over medium-high heat. Add the garlic, onion, and bell pepper; cook 2 minutes. Add the turkey and cook until no longer pink, about 2 minutes. Stir in the tomatoes, tomato paste, chili powder, cumin, oregano, salt, and cayenne; bring to a boil. Reduce the heat and simmer, stirring occasionally, until thickened, 15–18 minutes.

2 Bring a large pot of salted water to a boil. Add the pasta and cook according to package directions; drain. Serve the chili over the pasta.

What's for Lunch

Serve with an antipasto vegetable assortment, including carrot and celery sticks, and olives.

8 POINTS per serving

Per serving (1 cup):
412 Calories • 12 g Total Fat • 3 g Saturated Fat • 60 mg Cholesterol • 663 mg Sodium • 54 mg Total Carbohydrate
5 g Dietary Fiber • 23 g Protein • 88 mg Calcium

Asian Turkey Burgers with Quick Slaw

Makes 4 servings
(yield 5 cups)

4 cups thinly sliced Napa cabbage (about 3/4 pound)

2 carrots, shredded

1 red bell pepper, seeded and finely chopped

2 tablespoons rice vinegar

2 tablespoons chopped cilantro

1 1/2 tablespoons sugar

2 tablespoons reduced-sodium soy sauce

2 teaspoons Asian (dark) sesame oil

1 pound ground skinless turkey breast

2 tablespoons hoisin sauce

1 scallion, chopped

1 teaspoon ground ginger

4 English muffins, split and toasted

Soy sauce and sesame oil lend a distinctive Asian accent to these lean burgers and the snappy slaw that accompanies them. The burgers get an extra flavor boost from hoisin sauce and ginger, while the slaw is brimming with refreshing cilantro. Once the vegetables are prepped for the slaw, the meal will be ready in no time at all. Put some additional hoisin sauce on the side to garnish the burgers, if desired.

1 Preheat the broiler; spray the rack of a broiler pan with nonstick spray.

2 Combine the cabbage, carrots, bell pepper, vinegar, cilantro, sugar, 1 tablespoon of the soy sauce, and 1 teaspoon of the oil in a bowl. Toss to coat.

3 Combine the turkey, hoisin sauce, scallion, ginger, the remaining 1 tablespoon soy sauce, and the remaining 1 teaspoon oil in a second bowl. Shape into four 1/2-inch-thick patties. Transfer the patties to the broiler rack and broil, 4 inches from the heat, until cooked through, 4–5 minutes on each side. Place a patty on each of 4 English muffin halves and top each with one of the remaining muffin halves. Serve the cabbage slaw on the side.

What's for Lunch

Add an assortment of Asian pickles (available at an Asian grocery store) to the lunch table to continue the Far Eastern feel of this meal.

 COOK'S TIP The best way to mix ingredients for a burger is with your hands. Be sure to thoroughly wash your hands with warm water and soap for at least 30 seconds before and after handling the raw poultry.

7 POINTS per serving

Per serving (with generous 1 cup slaw):
348 Calories • 5 g Total Fat • 1 g Saturated Fat • 71 mg Cholesterol • 717 mg Sodium • 43 mg Total Carbohydrate
6 g Dietary Fiber • 33 g Protein • 183 mg Calcium

Smoky Black Bean Soup

A smoked turkey wing gives this soup its distinctive flavor. If you prefer your soup chunky, shred some of the turkey meat into the soup before serving. For a special presentation, garnish the soup with light sour cream and chopped red onion.

*Makes 6 servings
(yield 6 cups)*

1 tablespoon olive oil

3 garlic cloves, chopped

1 onion, chopped

1 green bell pepper, seeded and chopped

1 teaspoon ground cumin

1 teaspoon dried oregano

1 bay leaf

2 (15$\frac{1}{2}$-ounce) cans black beans, rinsed and drained

3 cups fat-free, reduced-sodium chicken broth

1 smoked turkey wing

$\frac{1}{4}$ teaspoon coarsely ground black pepper

 Heat the oil in a large saucepan over medium–high heat. Add the garlic, onion, bell pepper, cumin, oregano, and bay leaf. Cook, stirring occasionally, until the vegetables begin to soften, about 4 minutes. Add the beans, broth, turkey, and black pepper; bring to a boil. Cover, reduce the heat, and simmer 12 minutes.

 Discard the turkey wing and bay leaf. Puree the soup in a food processor or blender, in batches if necessary.

What's for Lunch

Superb with grilled ham and reduced-fat cheese sandwiches.

2 POINTS per serving

Per serving (1 cup):
135 Calories • 3 g Total Fat • 1 g Saturated Fat • 1 mg Cholesterol • 676 mg Sodium • 24 mg Total Carbohydrate
8 g Dietary Fiber • 8 g Protein • 72 mg Calcium

Thai Beef Noodle Salad

Thai fish sauce (you can also use very similar Vietnamese fish sauce), made from salted fermented anchovies, gives this dish its distinctive flavor. It can be found in Asian specialty stores and in many large supermarkets. In a pinch, substitute soy sauce for the fish sauce. Look in the same aisle of your market for the rice noodles, sometimes called cellophane noodles.

Makes 4 servings (yield 4 cups)

1 ounce rice noodles

3/4 pound beef top round steak, trimmed of all visible fat

1 large cucumber, peeled and thinly sliced

2 carrots, thinly sliced on the diagonal

1/2 cup thinly sliced red onion

1/4 cup sliced mint leaves

2 tablespoons fresh lime juice

2 tablespoons fish sauce

2 teaspoons sugar

1 Preheat the broiler. Coat the rack of a broiler pan with nonstick spray.

2 Put the noodles into a bowl and add sufficient boiling water to cover; let soak for 10 minutes. Rinse under cold running water, drain, and chop into 2-inch pieces.

3 Place the steak on the broiler rack and broil, 4 inches from the heat, until done to taste, 3 minutes on each side for medium-rare. Remove and let stand 5 minutes; thinly slice.

4 Combine the noodles, steak, cucumber, carrots, onion, mint, lime juice, fish sauce, and sugar in a large bowl; toss to mix.

What's for Lunch
Finish the meal with a fresh seasonal fruit salad.

 Lean inexpensive flank steak can be substituted for the beef top round.

Per serving:
184 Calories • 3 g Total Fat • 1 g Saturated Fat • 54 mg Cholesterol • 760 mg Sodium • 16 mg Total Carbohydrate
2 g Dietary Fiber • 22 g Protein • 44 mg Calcium

4 POINTS per serving

Canadian Bacon, Lettuce, and Tomato Sandwiches

In this low-fat rendition of the classic BLT, we use slices of Canadian bacon. Cut from the loin, rather than from the side of the pig, it is much leaner than typical bacon. For the best BLT, use crisp iceberg or romaine lettuce, freshly sliced tomato, and warm Canadian bacon.

Makes 4 servings

2 tablespoons light mayonnaise

1 tablespoon yellow mustard

1/4 teaspoon coarsely ground black pepper

8 slices whole-wheat bread

3/4 pound Canadian bacon

1 large tomato

4 lettuce leaves

1 Combine the mayonnaise, mustard, and pepper in a bowl.

2 Toast the bread in a toaster or toaster oven.

3 Cut the bacon into 12 slices. Heat a nonstick skillet over medium-high heat. Coat the skillet with nonstick spray and cook the bacon, in batches, until lightly brown and heated through, about 2 minutes on each side. Cover to keep warm.

4 Cut the tomato into 8 slices. Brush 4 slices of the toast with the mayonnaise mixture. Layer each slice with 1 lettuce leaf, 2 slices of tomato, and 3 slices bacon. Cover each sandwich with one of the remaining toast slices and cut the sandwiches in half on an angle.

What's for Lunch

These sandwiches go well with steaming mugs of split pea soup.

5 POINTS per serving

Per serving:
253 Calories • 8 g Total Fat • 3 g Saturated Fat • 41 mg Cholesterol • 1,360 mg Sodium • 28 mg Total Carbohydrate
4 g Dietary Fiber • 18 g Protein • 48 mg Calcium

Minestre Fagioli

Minestre is the Italian term for hearty soup boasting pasta or grains. We use tubetti in this filling version—which is brimming with such classic Italian flavors as fennel, prosciutto, tomatoes, and basil—but you could easily substitute ziti or any other short macaroni. The fagioli of choice for this recipe are cannellini, or white kidney beans.

Makes 6 servings
(yield 8 cups)

1 tablespoon olive oil

2 garlic cloves, chopped

1 celery stalk, chopped

1 carrot, chopped

1 onion, chopped

1/2 fennel bulb, chopped

1/4 pound deli-sliced prosciutto, chopped

1 (14 1/2-ounce) can whole peeled tomatoes, drained and chopped

4 cups fat-free, reduced-sodium chicken broth

2 (15 1/2-ounce) cans cannellini beans, rinsed and drained

1/4 pound tubetti

1/2 cup chopped fresh parsley

1/4 cup thinly sliced basil leaves

1/2 teaspoon salt

1/4 teaspoon coarsely ground black pepper

2 tablespoons grated Parmesan (optional)

Heat the oil in a large saucepan over medium-high heat. Add the garlic, celery, carrot, onion, fennel, and prosciutto; cook until the vegetables begin to soften, about 4 minutes. Add the tomatoes, broth, beans, and tubetti; bring to a boil and cook until the pasta is tender, about 8 minutes. Remove from the heat and stir in the parsley, basil, salt, and pepper. Sprinkle with Parmesan cheese if desired.

What's for Lunch

 Serve the soup with an assortment of breadsticks and some sliced melon for dessert.

COOK'S TIP This soup can also be made ahead. As is the case with many pasta and bean-based soups, it actually tastes better the next day, after the flavors have had a chance to meld. Either way it's comfort in a bowl.

5 *POINTS* per serving

Per serving (1 1/3 cups):
287 Calories • 5 g Total Fat • 1 g Saturated Fat • 13 mg Cholesterol • 1,380 mg Sodium • 43 g Total Carbohydrate
8 g Dietary Fiber • 17 g Protein • 114 mg Calcium

DINNER

Moroccan Vegetable Stew with Orange Couscous

The flavors of the Mediterranean—including aromatic fennel, nutty garbanzo beans, cinnamon, and cumin—grace this complex, but easily prepared, stew. It also boasts butternut squash, kale, and freshly grated ginger. Orange-infused couscous accompanies this pleasantly exotic stew.

Makes 4 servings (yield 6 cups stew and 3 cups couscous)

1 tablespoon olive oil

1 onion, thinly sliced

1 cup thinly sliced fennel bulb

1 tomato, chopped

3 carrots, sliced

1 teaspoon grated peeled fresh ginger

$1/2$ teaspoon ground cinnamon

$1/2$ teaspoon ground cumin

$1/2$ small butternut squash, cut into 2-inch chunks (about 2 cups)

2 (15-ounce) cans garbanzo beans, rinsed and drained

1 (10-ounce) package frozen chopped kale, thawed and squeezed dry

1 cup reduced-sodium chicken broth

$1^{3}/4$ cups water

2 tablespoons orange juice

2 teaspoons grated orange zest

1 tablespoon unsalted butter

$1/4$ teaspoon salt

1 (10-ounce) box quick-cooking couscous

1 tablespoon chopped fresh parsley

 1 Heat the oil in a large saucepan over medium heat. Add the onion, fennel, tomato, carrots, ginger, cinnamon, and cumin; cook until the vegetables begin to soften, about 8 minutes. Add the squash, garbanzo beans, kale, and broth; bring to a boil. Cover and simmer until the squash is tender, about 15 minutes.

 2 Combine the water, orange juice, orange zest, butter, and salt in a saucepan; bring to a boil. Stir in the couscous and parsley; cover and remove from the heat. Let stand until the liquid has been absorbed, about 5 minutes. Fluff the couscous with a fork.

 3 Transfer the stew to a bowl; serve with the couscous.

What's for Dinner

A refreshing cucumber salad rounds out the meal nicely.

 COOK'S TIP The fennel may be called anise in your market, and the garbanzo beans labeled as chickpeas.

12 POINTS per serving

Per serving (1 1/2 cups):
616 Calories • 10 g Total Fat • 3 g Saturated Fat • 8 mg Cholesterol • 722 mg Sodium • 109 mg Total Carbohydrate 18 g Dietary Fiber • 24 g Protein • 261 mg Calcium

Curried Quinoa with Green Beans, Carrots, and Scallions

Quinoa is a South American grain, new to the North American market. Touted as a "wonder grain" quinoa is a complete protein, meaning it contains all eight essential amino acids. Serve this curry warm or at room temperature.

*Makes 4 servings
(yield 5 cups)*

1 cup quinoa, rinsed well under warm running water and drained

1 cup orange juice

1 cup water

1 tablespoon curry powder

1 teaspoon ground coriander

3/4 teaspoon salt

1/4 teaspoon ground cinnamon

1/2 pound green beans, trimmed and halved crosswise

2 teaspoons olive oil

2 carrots, sliced

1 onion, chopped

1/4 cup sliced almonds

1/2 cup raisins

2 large scallions, chopped

3 tablespoons chopped fresh mint

2 tablespoons fresh lemon juice

1 teaspoon grated lemon zest

1 Combine the quinoa, orange juice, water, curry powder, coriander, salt, and cinnamon in a saucepan; bring to a boil. Cover, reduce the heat, and simmer until all of the liquid has been absorbed, 12–15 minutes.

2 Bring a large saucepan of salted water to a boil. Add the green beans and cook 3 minutes; drain and transfer to a large bowl.

3 Heat the oil in a nonstick skillet over medium-high heat. Add the carrots and onion and cook until they begin to soften, about 3 minutes; stir in the almonds and cook 2 minutes longer. Transfer the contents of the skillet to the bowl with the green beans. Add the raisins, scallions, mint, lemon juice, lemon zest, and quinoa. Stir to mix.

What's for Dinner

This quinoa salad nicely accompanies roast and chicken dishes. For a vegetarian meal, serve with a green salad.

 COOK'S TIP Remember to rinse quinoa well in warm water before cooking to remove its bitter-tasting coating.

7 POINTS per serving

Per serving:
355 Calories • 9 g Total Fat • 1 g Saturated Fat • 0 mg Cholesterol • 466 mg Sodium • 63 mg Total Carbohydrate
9 g Dietary Fiber • 10 g Protein • 118 mg Calcium

Vegetarian Chili

We usually think of chocolate as a confection or dessert. In Mexico, however, chocolate is commonly used in savory dishes, such as chicken in mole sauce, to give added depth of flavor. A combination of cocoa powder and chocolate is used in this dish to achieve a similar result.

Makes 4 servings
(yield 6 cups)

1 tablespoon canola oil

2 garlic cloves, chopped

1 large onion, chopped

1 green bell pepper, seeded and chopped

1 jalapeño pepper, seeded and chopped (wear gloves to prevent irritation)

2 (15$1/2$-ounce) cans red kidney beans, rinsed and drained

1 (28-ounce) can whole peeled tomatoes, drained and chopped

1 (10-ounce) package frozen corn kernels, thawed

1 tablespoon chili powder

1 tablespoon cocoa powder

1 teaspoon dried oregano

$1/2$ teaspoon salt

$1/4$ teaspoon coarsely ground black pepper

1 ounce semi-sweet chocolate

Heat the oil in a large saucepan over medium-high heat. Add the garlic, onion, bell pepper, and jalapeño pepper; cook, stirring often, until the vegetables begin to soften, 4–5 minutes. Add the beans, tomatoes, corn, chili powder, cocoa powder, oregano, salt, and black pepper. Bring to a boil and cook, stirring often to prevent scorching, until beginning to thicken slightly, about 15 minutes. Remove from the heat and add the chocolate, stirring until melted.

What's for Dinner

Garnish the chili with chopped onion and light sour cream and serve with plenty of cornbread on the side.

8 *POINTS* per serving

Per serving (1$1/2$ cups):
385 Calories • 8 g Total Fat • 2 g Saturated Fat • 0 mg Cholesterol • 1,050 mg Sodium • 69 mg Total Carbohydrate
20 g Dietary Fiber • 17 g Protein • 138 mg Calcium

Vegetarian Chili

Eggplant and Tofu with Garlic Sauce

Healthy and tasty, this easy dish can be made in a flash once the ingredients have been prepped. Be sure to use firm tofu; soft or silken tofu would fall apart over the fairly high heat used in this recipe.

Makes 4 servings

²/3 cup reduced-sodium chicken broth

3 tablespoons red wine vinegar

3 tablespoons reduced-sodium soy sauce

2 tablespoons sugar

1 tablespoon cornstarch

2 teaspoons Asian (dark) sesame oil

3 garlic cloves, minced

1 teaspoon grated peeled fresh ginger

1 teaspoon canola oil

4 small eggplant (about 1 pound), halved lengthwise

6 scallions, cut into 2-inch slices

1 pound firm tofu, cut into 2-inch chunks

1 Whisk together the broth, vinegar, soy sauce, sugar, cornstarch, sesame oil, garlic, and ginger in a bowl.

2 Heat the canola oil in a large nonstick skillet over medium–high heat. Add the eggplant and scallions. Cover and cook, turning the eggplant occasionally, until it begins to soften slightly, about 10 minutes. Add the broth mixture; bring to a boil. Boil until the sauce begins to thicken, about 1 minute. Stir in the tofu.

What's for Dinner

 This is terrific over brown or wild rice.

4·POINTS per serving

Per serving:
199 Calories • 9 g Total Fat • 1 g Saturated Fat • 0 mg Cholesterol • 515 mg Sodium • 21 mg Total Carbohydrate
3 g Dietary Fiber • 12 g Protein • 216 mg Calcium

Spinach Lasagna

A favorite one-dish meal, lasagna is an ideal—and often overlooked—lunch or brunch option. It can be easily dressed up or down with accompanying dishes, and it makes a great buffet addition. For this quick and easy recipe, look for no-boil noodles to save time.

Makes 6 servings

1 tablespoon olive oil

1/4 cup finely chopped onion

3 tablespoons all-purpose flour

4 cups low-fat (1%) milk

1 (15-ounce) container fat-free ricotta cheese

1 (10-ounce) package frozen chopped spinach, thawed and squeezed dry

1 egg white

1/4 teaspoon ground nutmeg

9 no-boil lasagna noodles

1 Preheat the oven to 400°F.

2 Heat the oil in a nonstick saucepan over medium-high heat. Add the onion and cook until slightly wilted, about 3 minutes. Add the flour, stirring until blended. Whisk in the milk and bring to a boil. Boil until the white sauce thickens, about 5 minutes. Remove from the heat.

3 Meanwhile, combine the ricotta cheese, spinach, egg white, and nutmeg in a bowl. Spoon 1 cup of the sauce onto the bottom of an 11 × 7-inch baking dish. Arrange 3 noodles over the sauce. Spread one-half of the ricotta mixture evenly over the noodles. Top with 1 cup sauce. Layer 3 more noodles, the remaining ricotta mixture, and 1 cup sauce. Top with the remaining noodles and sauce. Bake, uncovered, until hot and bubbly, 20–25 minutes.

What's for Dinner

Serve with crusty Italian bread, a side mesclun salad and a jug of red wine.

 To quickly thaw spinach, place the spinach from a ten-ounce package in a microwavable bowl with a cover and microwave on High two minutes. With a knife, break up the spinach and microwave on High one minute longer.

6 POINTS per serving

Per serving:
279 Calories • 5 g Total Fat • 2 g Saturated Fat • 13 mg Cholesterol • 297 mg Sodium • 36 mg Total Carbohydrate • 1 g Dietary Fiber • 21 g Protein • 544 mg Calcium

DINNER

Wild Mushroom Risotto

Ever-popular as a first course in Italy, especially in the North where rice grows abundantly, risotto has caught on with American diners in recent years. In addition to being a main course, this dish is a welcome buffet addition.

Makes 6 servings

6 cups fat-free, reduced-sodium chicken broth

1 tablespoon olive oil

1 shallot, chopped

2 garlic cloves, chopped

2 1/2 cups sliced wild mushrooms

1/4 teaspoon dried thyme

1 1/2 cups arborio rice

1/2 cup dry sherry

1/2 cup grated Parmesan cheese

1/4 teaspoon coarsely ground black pepper

 1 Bring the broth to a boil in a large saucepan. Reduce the heat to keep at a simmer.

2 Heat the oil in a large nonstick skillet over medium-high heat. Add the shallot and garlic and cook 1 minute. Add the mushrooms and thyme and cook until the mushrooms begin to soften, about 4 minutes. Add the rice and cook 30 seconds. Add the sherry and cook, stirring constantly, until almost absorbed, about 1 minute. Add the broth, 1 cup at a time, stirring until it is absorbed before adding more, until the rice is just tender. (You may not need to add all 6 cups.) The cooking time from the first addition of broth should be 18–20 minutes. Stir in the Parmesan cheese and pepper; serve at once.

What's for Dinner

 All you need to add is a simple spinach or arugula salad.

COOK'S TIP Leftover risotto is wonderful served up in the form of risotto cakes. Simply mix the leftover risotto with enough egg white and plain dried bread crumbs so that it can be easily shaped into patties. Coat the cakes in some more bread crumbs and bake in a shallow pan, in a preheated 400°F oven, until heated through and lightly crisp on the outside.

Per serving:
302 Calories • 4 g Total Fat • 2 g Saturated Fat • 5 mg Cholesterol • 681 mg Sodium • 50 mg Total Carbohydrate
1 g Dietary Fiber • 11 g Protein • 133 mg Calcium

6 POINTS per serving

Penne with Eggplant, Zucchini, and Yellow Squash

Make sure to cut the vegetables for this party pasta dish about the same size, so they will cook evenly. For a summer pasta salad, add chopped tomato and chopped arugula or watercress. Bow tie pasta can easily replace the penne.

Makes 8 servings
(yield 10 cups)

1 (1-pound) eggplant, cut into 1-inch cubes

2 (6-ounce) zucchini, cut into 1-inch cubes

2 (6-ounce) yellow squash, cut into 1-inch cubes

1 onion, cut into 1-inch cubes

1 red bell pepper, seeded and cut into 1-inch cubes

3/4 pound penne

1/2 cup chopped fresh basil

1/4 cup grated Parmesan cheese

2 tablespoons extra-virgin olive oil

1 Preheat the broiler. Spray 2 baking pans with nonstick spray.

2 Place the eggplant, zucchini, yellow squash, onion, and bell pepper in a single layer on the baking pans; spray to coat well with nonstick spray. Broil, 7 inches from the heat, until the vegetables are tender and browned, 15–20 minutes. Transfer to a large bowl.

3 Bring a large pot of water to a boil. Add the penne and cook according to package directions; drain, and add to the bowl with the vegetables. Add the basil, Parmesan cheese, and oil; toss to coat.

What's for Dinner

Serve with grilled sausages on the side; for a vegetarian meal, try with sliced grilled wild mushrooms.

 COOK'S TIP Depending upon the size of your broiler, you may need to broil the vegetables, one baking sheet at a time. Or, roast the vegetables in a 500°F oven 20 minutes, until tender and browned.

Per serving:

4 POINTS per serving

236 Calories • 5 g Total Fat • 1 g Saturated Fat • 2 mg Cholesterol • 54 mg Sodium • 40 mg Total Carbohydrate
4 g Dietary Fiber • 8 g Protein • 69 mg Calcium

DINNER

Polenta with Wild Mushrooms

Dried mushrooms, such as the porcinis used in this mushroom lover's delight, have an earthy taste and chewy texture that add depth to any dish. They must be rehydrated in hot water for a few minutes before using; the soaking liquid becomes a rich flavorful mushroom broth that can be added to your recipe.

Makes 4 servings

1 tablespoon dried porcini mushrooms

1 cup hot water

1 teaspoon olive oil

1 onion, chopped

2 garlic cloves, minced

1 tomato, chopped

1/4 cup sliced white mushrooms

1/4 cup sliced cremini mushrooms

1/4 cup sliced oyster mushrooms

1/4 cup sliced shiitake mushrooms

1/4 cup dry white wine

6 oil-cured black olives, pitted and chopped

1 tablespoon chopped fresh thyme, or 1 teaspoon dried

3 cups water

2/3 cup quick-cooking polenta

1 tablespoon butter

3 tablespoons grated Parmesan cheese

 Place the porcini mushrooms in a small bowl; cover with the hot water and let stand 10 minutes. Drain, reserving the soaking liquid, and coarsely chop.

 Heat the oil in a large nonstick skillet over medium heat. Add the onion and garlic; cook until the garlic is fragrant and the onion tender, about 5 minutes. Stir in the tomato, the porcinis, and the white, cremini, oyster, and shiitake mushrooms. Simmer, uncovered, until the mushrooms are tender, about 10 minutes. Add the wine, olives, thyme, and reserved mushroom liquid; bring to a boil. Cook, uncovered, until the liquid is reduced by half and the mushrooms are tender, about 5 minutes longer. Remove from the heat and cover to keep warm.

 Bring the 3 cups water to a boil in a saucepan. While whisking, sprinkle in the polenta. Cook, stirring frequently with a wooden spoon, until very thick, about 5 minutes. Remove from the heat and stir in the butter and Parmesan cheese.

 Serve the mushrooms over the polenta.

What's for Dinner

Pick up a cooked chicken to complete this meal.

 Shiitake, oyster, and crimini mushrooms are now available in a mixed bag in many markets.

4 POINTS per serving

Per serving:
194 Calories • 6 g Total Fat • 3 g Saturated Fat • 11 mg Cholesterol • 159 mg Sodium • 29 mg Total Carbohydrate 3 g Dietary Fiber • 5 g Protein • 72 mg Calcium

Seared Cod with Chunky Eggplant Sauce

Mild cod takes well to robust sauces, such as this eggplant sauce seasoned with tomatoes, olives, and fresh basil. The sauce is very versatile and goes well with many other types of fish, as well as with chicken or pasta.

Makes 4 servings
(yield 1¹/2 cups sauce)

2 teaspoons olive oil

4 (6-ounce) cod fillets

1 (¹/2-pound) pound eggplant, cut into 1-inch chunks

¹/4 cup water

1 (14¹/2-ounce) can peeled Italian tomatoes, with their juice

¹/4 cup dry white wine

10 kalamata olives, pitted and coarsely chopped

¹/2 teaspoon salt

¹/2 teaspoon sugar

¹/2 cup chopped fresh basil

1 Heat 1 teaspoon of the oil in a large nonstick skillet over medium-high heat. Sauté the cod until browned on both sides, about 6 minutes; transfer to a plate.

2 Add the remaining 1 teaspoon oil to the skillet. Stir in the eggplant and water. Cook until the eggplant begins to soften and brown, about 4 minutes. Add the tomatoes, wine, olives, salt, and sugar, stirring with a wooden spoon to break up the tomatoes. Cover, reduce the heat, and simmer about 10 minutes to blend the flavors. Stir in the basil. Return the cod to the skillet briefly to heat through.

What's for Dinner

Serve with sweet potato fries that you can make yourself. Toss sweet potatoes that have been peeled and cut into ¹/4-inch thick sticks with just enough canola oil to coat and bake in a preheated 500°F oven until golden, turning once, about 20 minutes.

COOK'S TIP Cod fillets from a large cod can be quite big. If you buy one very large fillet, simply cut it into four equal pieces.

---

4 POINTS per serving

Per serving (with about ¹/3 cup sauce):
206 Calories • 5 g Total Fat • 1 g Saturated Fat • /3 mg Cholesterol • 655 mg Sodium • 8 mg Total Carbohydrate
2 g Dietary Fiber • 32 g Protein • 65 mg Calcium

Louisiana-Style Flounder

This dish gets its character from the classic aromatic "trinity" that is the core of traditional Cajun and Creole cooking: onion, green bell pepper, and celery. Mild tasting flounder makes a nice foil to this robust seasoning blend.

Makes 4 servings
(yield 1 cup sauce)

1 tablespoon olive oil

1/2 cup chopped onion

1/2 cup seeded and chopped green bell pepper

1 celery stalk, chopped

2 tablespoons Cajun seasoning

1 tomato, finely chopped

1 garlic clove, chopped

1 tablespoon chopped fresh thyme, or 1 teaspoon dried

1/2 teaspoon salt

4 (4-ounce) flounder fillets

 Heat 2 teaspoons of the oil in a nonstick saucepan over medium-low heat. Add the onion, bell pepper, celery, and 1 tablespoon of the Cajun seasoning. Cover and simmer until the vegetables are very tender, about 8 minutes. Add the tomato, garlic, thyme, and salt. Continue to cook, uncovered, until the tomato is very soft, about 5 minutes longer.

2 Sprinkle the fish with the remaining 1 tablespoon Cajun seasoning. Heat the remaining 1 teaspoon oil in a skillet over medium heat. Add the fish and cook until just opaque in center, about 3 minutes on each side. Transfer the fillets to a platter and spoon the sauce over the fish.

What's for Dinner

Steamed okra and rice complement the fish nicely.

3 POINTS per serving

Per serving (1 filet with 1/4 cup sauce):
160 Calories • 5 g Total Fat • 1 g Saturated Fat • 63 mg Cholesterol • 1,210 mg Sodium • 5 mg Total Carbohydrate
1 g Dietary Fiber • 23 g Protein • 32 mg Calcium

Lemon Crumb Fillet of Sole

Fresh bread crumbs really make the difference in this recipe. Flounder, red snapper, catfish, cod, or any white fish works well in place of the sole

Makes 4 servings

4 slices thinly sliced white bread

2 teaspoons grated lemon zest

2 tablespoons coarse-grained Dijon mustard

1 tablespoon fresh lemon juice

4 (5-ounce) sole fillets

1/2 teaspoon salt

1/2 teaspoon coarsely ground black pepper

1 Preheat the oven to 425°F.

2 Combine the bread and lemon zest in a food processor; pulse to form coarse crumbs. Mix together the mustard and lemon juice in a small bowl.

3 Spray a baking pan with nonstick spray. Sprinkle both sides of the fillets with the salt and pepper and place them in the pan. Brush with the mustard mixture; top with the bread crumbs, pressing down so that the crumbs adhere. Spray lightly with nonstick spray. Bake until the coating is golden and the fish just opaque in the center, about 8 minutes.

What's for Dinner

 Serve the fish with sautéed spinach and cherry tomato halves.

COOK'S TIP Do not turn the fillets during baking. Many thin cuts of fish, such as these, should be baked or broiled on only one side since turning can cause them to dry out and fall apart.

4 POINTS per serving

Per serving:
199 Calories • 3 g Total Fat • 1 g Saturated Fat • 77 mg Cholesterol • 560 mg Sodium • 11 mg Total Carbohydrate
1 g Dietary Fiber • 30 g Protein • 55 mg Calcium

Tuna Panzanella

Panzanella is the traditional Italian bread salad that makes the most of leftover bread. The addition of tuna makes it a filling main dish. Once you've done the chopping and slicing, it's a cinch.

*Makes 6 servings
(yield 12 cups)*

8 ounces thick-crusted Italian bread (about 1/2 loaf), cut into 3/4-inch cubes

1 1/2 pounds ripe tomatoes, seeded and roughly chopped

1/2 cup thinly sliced red onion

1 cucumber, peeled, halved lengthwise, seeded, and sliced

2 (6-ounce) cans solid white tuna in water, drained

3 tablespoons extra-virgin olive oil

2 tablespoons red wine vinegar

1/2 cup sliced basil leaves

1/2 teaspoon salt

1/2 teaspoon coarsely ground black pepper

Combine the bread cubes, tomatoes, onion, cucumber, tuna, oil, vinegar, basil, salt, and pepper in a large bowl. Toss well to combine and let stand 10 minutes before serving.

What's for Dinner

For a convenient summer supper of salads, serve with a crisp bagged mesclun salad with a vinaigrette dressing.

 COOK'S TIP For best results, use day-old bread.

5 POINTS per serving

Per serving:
255 Calories • 9 g Total Fat • 1 g Saturated Fat • 21 mg Cholesterol • 635 mg Sodium • 26 mg Total Carbohydrate
3 g Dietary Fiber • 17 g Protein • 53 mg Calcium

Moules Marinière

These steamed mussels are a French classic closely associated with the Provençal region. Mussels attach themselves to rocks with small hair-like cords known as beards. Before cooking a mussel, simply grab the beard between your fingers and twist it to remove. Or, buy debearded mussels, if they are available from your fish merchant.

Makes 2 servings

3/4 cup dry white wine

4 garlic cloves, chopped

1 tomato, chopped

1/2 cup chopped fresh parsley

1 sprig thyme

1/2 bay leaf

1/4 teaspoon coarsely ground black pepper

1/4 teaspoon crushed red pepper

3 pounds mussels, scrubbed and debearded

Combine the wine, garlic, tomato, parsley, thyme, bay leaf, black pepper, and crushed red pepper in a large pot over medium-high heat. Bring to a boil, add the mussels, and cover. Cook, shaking the pot, until the mussels open, 7–9 minutes. Discard the bay leaf. Serve in bowls with some of the cooking juices.

What's for Dinner

All you need is a side salad and a loaf of hearty bread with which to sop up the broth.

 Test to see that the mussel is still alive and fresh by tapping on the shell. Live mussels will close when tapped or when being rinsed. Discard any mussels that do not close when being rinsed or do not open while steaming.

Per serving:
241 Calories • 5 g Total Fat • 1 g Saturated Fat • 64 mg Cholesterol • 669 mg Sodium • 15 mg Total Carbohydrate
1 g Dietary Fiber • 29 g Protein • 97 mg Calcium

5 *POINTS* per serving

Lemon Pepper Cod

A simple lemon and garlic marinade and a sprinkle of herbs and seasonings lends lots of zest to baked cod fillets in this recipe. You could easily substitute scrod, hake, haddock, or pollock for the cod.

Makes 4 servings

3 tablespoons fresh lemon juice

1 garlic clove, minced

4 (6-ounce) cod fillets

1/4 cup chopped fresh parsley

1 tablespoon olive oil

2 teaspoons grated lemon zest

3/4 teaspoon salt

1/2 teaspoon coarsely ground black pepper

1 Preheat the oven to 450°F. Coat a baking sheet with nonstick spray.

2 Combine the lemon juice and garlic in a large, shallow bowl. Add the cod fillets, turn to coat, and let stand 10 minutes.

3 In another bowl, combine the parsley, oil, lemon zest, salt, and pepper. Transfer the cod fillets to the baking sheet and press an equal amount of the parsley mixture onto each fillet. Bake until the fish is just opaque in the center, 8–10 minutes.

What's for Dinner

 Keep it simple and serve the fish with parslied small red potatoes and green beans.

 COOK'S TIP Boil small red potatoes, with their skins left on, in boiling salted water about 15 minutes, or until tender. Drain the potatoes and toss with one teaspoon of butter and a handful of chopped fresh parsley. Jazz up the flavor with a lemon wedge

4 POINTS per serving

Per serving:
178 Calories • 5 g Total Fat • 1 g Saturated Fat • 74 mg Cholesterol • 544 mg Sodium • 2 mg Total Carbohydrate
0 g Dietary Fiber • 31 g Protein • 29 mg Calcium

Poached Salmon with Dill Mustard Sauce

There's so much you can do with poached salmon: plate it hot and drizzle with sauce, serve it cold on a buffet, or flake it into a summer salad. Here, it's served on baby greens and drizzled with a classic dill mustard sauce.

Makes 4 servings

1 (8-ounce) bottle clam juice

1 cup water

1 onion, chopped

1 carrot, chopped

1 celery stalk, chopped

1 bay leaf

4 (6-ounce) salmon fillets, skin removed

$1/2$ cup fat-free mayonnaise

2 tablespoons chopped fresh dill

1 tablespoon Dijon mustard

1 tablespoon fresh lemon juice

$1/8$ teaspoon coarsely ground black pepper

8 cups baby spinach, cleaned and left damp

$1/4$ teaspoon salt

1. Combine the clam juice, water, onion, carrot, celery, and bay leaf in a skillet; bring to a boil over high heat. Cover, reduce the heat to medium, and simmer 5 minutes. Add the salmon and cook 6 minutes. Turn the fillets over and cook until just opaque in the center, about 3 minutes longer. Transfer to a plate and cover to keep warm.

2. Combine the mayonnaise, dill, mustard, lemon juice, and pepper in a small bowl.

3. Heat a nonstick skillet over medium–high heat. Add the spinach and cook just until wilted, about 1 minute. Stir in the salt. Divide the spinach among 4 dinner plates, place a piece of salmon on each, and drizzle with the sauce.

What's for Dinner

 Serve with steamed green beans and dilled new potatoes.

COOK'S TIP To make the dilled potatoes, cook new potatoes in boiling salted water; drain and toss with fat-free sour cream and chopped fresh dill.

5 *POINTS* per serving

Per serving:
236 Calories • 8 g Total Fat • 2 g Saturated Fat • 93 mg Cholesterol • 550 mg Sodium • 7 mg Total Carbohydrate
6 g Dietary Fiber • 36 g Protein • 99 mg Calcium

Grilled Salmon Roulade with Lemon-Dill Aïoli

These elegantly rolled salmon steaks are finished with aïoli, the classic garlic-based mayonnaise of the Mediterranean. When you mash the garlic for the aïoli, cut each clove in half and sprinkle with coarse kosher salt; this helps pulverize the garlic. The salmon takes naturally to the grill, but can just as easily be broiled.

Makes 4 servings (yield 1/3 cup aïoli)

4 (6-ounce) salmon steaks

2 teaspoons olive oil

1/2 teaspoon salt

1/2 teaspoon coarsely ground black pepper

1/4 cup reduced-calorie mayonnaise

1 garlic clove, mashed to a paste

1 tablespoon low-fat (1%) milk

1 teaspoon grated lemon zest

1 1/2 teaspoons fresh lemon juice

1 1/2 teaspoons chopped fresh dill

 1 Preheat the grill or broiler.

2 Remove the bone from inside the cavity of each steak with the tip of a knife and trim about 1 inch off each outer flap. Roll one flap of each steak into the cavity, then roll the other flap around the outside and secure loosely with kitchen twine. Rub with the oil and sprinkle with the salt and pepper. Grill or broil (4 inches from the heat, on the rack of a broiler pan sprayed with nonstick spray) the salmon until just opaque in the center, about 5 minutes on each side.

3 Combine the mayonnaise, garlic, milk, lemon zest, lemon juice, and dill in a small bowl, stirring to blend thoroughly. Spoon over the salmon.

What's for Dinner

To counteract this rich main dish, serve the salmon with brown rice, tossed with very thin strips of sweet red bell pepper and zucchini.

 COOK'S TIP For the same wonderful taste in a quicker workday package, simply grill or broil four 6-ounce salmon fillets for about five minutes on each side, and top with the aïoli.

8 *POINTS* per serving

Per serving:
312 Calories • 20g Total Fat • 4g Saturated Fat • 85 mg Cholesterol • 501 mg Sodium • 2 mg Total Carbohydrate
0 g Dietary Fiber • 28 g Protein • 27 mg Calcium

Scallops with Salsa Cruda

Salsa cruda is a raw tomato sauce that cooks just slightly from the heat of the pasta. For simple variations on this dish, substitute shrimp or sautéed chicken for the scallops.

*Makes 4 servings
(yield 4 cups)*

1¹/2 pounds ripe tomatoes, seeded and chopped

¹/2 cup chopped fresh basil

¹/2 cup chopped fresh parsley

¹/2 cup finely chopped onion

3 tablespoons extra-virgin olive oil

2 tablespoons balsamic vinegar

1 garlic clove, minced

³/4 teaspoon salt

¹/2 teaspoon coarsely ground black pepper

¹/2 pound medium-size pasta shells

1 pound bay scallops

 Combine the tomatoes, basil, parsley, onion, 2 ¹/2 tablespoons of the oil, the vinegar, garlic, ¹/2 teaspoon of the salt, and ¹/4 teaspoon of the pepper in a large bowl.

2 Bring a large pot of salted water to a boil. Add the pasta shells and cook according to package directions. Drain and add to the bowl with the sauce; toss to coat.

3 Heat the remaining ¹/2 tablespoon oil in a large nonstick skillet over medium–high heat. Sprinkle the scallops with the remaining ¹/4 teaspoon salt and ¹/4 teaspoon pepper and add to the skillet. Cook, shaking the skillet occasionally, until the scallops are lightly browned and cooked through, 3–5 minutes. Transfer to the bowl with the pasta mixture and mix well.

What's for Dinner

Pair this light dish with red chard that has been sautéed in balsamic vinegar.

 When bay scallops are in season, they're unbeatable for flavor; otherwise, use quartered sea scallops.

9 *POINTS* per serving

Per serving:
447 Calories • 13 g Total Fat • 2 g Saturated Fat • 37 mg Cholesterol • 715 mg Sodium • 55 mg Total Carbohydrate
4 g Dietary Fiber • 28 g Protein • 67 mg Calcium

DINNER

Seared Scallops on Scallion Orzo

*Makes 4 servings
(yield 3 cups orzo)*

1 cup orzo

2 tablespoons olive oil

2 garlic cloves, sliced

1 red bell pepper, seeded and finely chopped

1 cup chopped scallions (about 8–10 scallions)

2 tablespoons fresh lemon juice

1 teaspoon salt

1 pound sea scallops

2 teaspoons cracked black pepper

When purchasing scallops, look for a moist sheen and a fresh sweet scent. Refrigerate as soon as you bring them home, and use within two days. For this quick and easy stovetop presentation, be sure to thoroughly pat the scallops dry after you rinse them. Moist scallops will steam and can stick to the skillet, rather than sear.

1 Bring a pot of salted water to a boil. Add the orzo and cook according to package directions; drain.

2 Heat 1½ tablespoons of the oil in a nonstick skillet over medium-high heat. Add the garlic and cook 1 minute. Stir in the bell pepper and cook 2 minutes. Add the scallions and cook until wilted, about 30 seconds. Remove from the heat and add the orzo, lemon juice, and ½ teaspoon of the salt; cover to keep warm.

3 Heat the remaining ½ tablespoon oil in a large nonstick skillet over medium-high heat. Sprinkle the scallops with the remaining ½ teaspoon salt and the black pepper. Add to the skillet and cook until lightly browned and opaque, 3–4 minutes on each side. Serve over the orzo.

What's for Dinner

 Serve with a sophisticated side dish of sautéed fennel and radicchio.

COOK'S TIP Some imported brands of orzo come without directions; cook as you would any other pasta, testing for doneness after about eight minutes.

7 POINTS **per serving**

Per serving (with ¾ cup orzo):
342 Calories • 8 g Total Fat • 1 g Saturated Fat • 37 mg Cholesterol • 845 mg Sodium • 41 mg Total Carbohydrate
3 g Dietary Fiber • 26 g Protein • 64 mg Calcium

Herb-Crusted Shrimp

A refreshing alternative to battered and fried shrimp, these tasty morsels are delicious hot or at room temperature, making them an ideal buffet item. The time-consuming part of this recipe is the prepping: Chop the assortment of fresh herbs that lend the dish its distinctive flavor ahead of time and the cooking will be done in just a few minutes.

Makes 4 servings

¹/4 cup chopped fresh basil

¹/4 cup chopped fresh mint

¹/4 cup chopped fresh parsley

¹/4 cup chopped cilantro

2 garlic cloves, minced

2 tablespoons fresh lemon juice

1 tablespoon olive oil

¹/2 teaspoon salt

¹/4 teaspoon coarsely ground black pepper

1¹/2 pounds large shrimp, peeled and deveined

 Preheat the oven to 450°F. Coat a baking sheet with nonstick spray.

 Combine the basil, mint, parsley, cilantro, garlic, lemon juice, oil, salt, and pepper in a bowl. Add the shrimp and toss to coat.

3 Arrange the shrimp in a single layer on a baking sheet. Bake until opaque and cooked through, about 6 minutes.

What's for Dinner

Oven-baked fries and a zesty coleslaw round out this menu nicely.

 COOK'S TIP For an hors d'oeuvre, thread each shrimp onto a short bamboo skewer and serve with a dipping sauce of nonfat mayonnaise mixed with chopped capers, lemon juice, and grated lemon zest.

4 POINTS per serving

Per serving:
176 Calories • 5 g Total Fat • 1 g Saturated Fat • 269 mg Cholesterol • 607 mg Sodium • 2 mg Total Carbohydrate
1 g Dietary Fiber • 29 g Protein • 81 mg Calcium

DINNER

Bourbon Barbecued Shrimp with Pecan Rice

Makes 4 servings

1 teaspoon canola oil

1/2 cup chopped onion

1 cup converted white rice

1 1/2 cups reduced-sodium chicken broth

1/4 cup chopped pecans, toasted

2 tablespoons chopped fresh parsley

1/4 cup steak sauce

3 tablespoons cider vinegar

3 tablespoons ketchup

3 tablespoons packed light brown sugar

2 tablespoons bourbon

1 teaspoon hot pepper sauce

1 pound medium shrimp, shelled and deveined

We sauté the rice until it's golden brown to give it a toasted, nutty flavor, which is then accentuated by the toasted pecans. When toasting nuts, heat them in a dry skillet over low heat, shaking the skillet often, until they are golden brown; immediately transfer to a bowl to prevent them from burning from residual heat from the skillet.

1 Heat the oil in a nonstick saucepan over medium heat. Add the onion and cook until tender and golden, about 5 minutes. Add the rice, stirring to coat well, and cook until it begins to turn golden, about 3 minutes. Add the broth and bring to a boil. Cover, reduce the heat, and simmer until the broth has evaporated and the rice is tender, about 20 minutes. Remove from heat and stir in the pecans and parsley.

2 Mix the steak sauce, vinegar, ketchup, brown sugar, bourbon, and pepper sauce in a bowl until blended. Add the shrimp and toss to coat.

3 Heat a nonstick, ridged grill pan over medium-high heat. Grill the shrimp until pink and lightly browned, about 3 minutes. Turn the shrimp and cook until nicely browned, about 2 minutes longer. Spoon the rice onto a platter and top with the shrimp.

What's for Dinner

A carrot and raisin salad is the perfect complement for this spicy meal.

 COOK'S TIP Making your own barbecue sauce is not only easy, but allows you to control the heat as well. For extra spicy sauce, add some chopped jalapeños, crushed red pepper, or a few extra drops of hot pepper sauce.

Per serving:
391 Calories • 8 g Total Fat • 1 g Saturated Fat • 140 mg Cholesterol • 616 mg Sodium • 53 mg Total Carbohydrate
2 g Dietary Fiber • 25 g Protein • 94 mg Calcium

8 POINTS per serving

Spicy Thai Seafood Supper

Today's mussels are often farm-raised, so they no longer require time-consuming scrubbing and debearding. However, do discard any mussels that do not shut when rinsed or that do not open when cooked.

Makes 4 servings

1 teaspoon canola oil

1 tablespoon grated peeled fresh ginger

1 garlic clove, minced

1 tablespoon Thai red curry paste

1 tablespoon packed light brown sugar

1 (14-ounce) can light coconut milk

$^1/_2$ cup water

1 tablespoon fish sauce

1 dozen littleneck clams, cleaned

1 dozen mussels, scrubbed and debearded

$^1/_2$ pound small shrimp, peeled and deveined

$^1/_2$ cup chopped fresh basil

1 Heat the oil in a large sauté pan over low heat. Add the ginger and garlic and cook until fragrant, about 1 minute. Stir in the red curry paste and brown sugar; cook 1 minute. Add the coconut milk, water, and fish sauce; bring to a boil. Simmer, uncovered, until the sauce thickens slightly, about 8 minutes.

2 Add the clams, cover, and simmer until they are just beginning to open, about 5 minutes. Add the mussels, shrimp, and basil. Continue to cook until the mussels open and the shrimp turn pink, 2–3 minutes longer.

What's for Dinner

 Serve with Chinese broccoli and steamed rice.

 COOK'S TIP Fish sauce, used in many Thai recipes, is pungent and robustly flavorful; a little goes a long way. It can be found in Asian markets and larger supermarkets.

6 *POINTS* per serving

Per serving:
232 Calories • 12 g Total Fat • 6 g Saturated Fat • 93 mg Cholesterol • 622 mg Sodium • 9 mg Total Carbohydrate
0 g Dietary Fiber • 20 g Protein • 101 mg Calcium

Easy Paella

A national favorite in Spain, paella is traditionally made with long-cooking arborio or Valencia rice; we use long-grain white rice in this rendition to speed up the cooking. You could substitute clams for the mussels, allowing five to ten minutes more steaming time.

*Makes 4 servings
(yield about 8 cups)*

3 slices bacon, cut into
$^1/_2$-inch pieces

3 garlic cloves, chopped

1 yellow onion, chopped

1 red bell pepper, seeded
and chopped

1 green bell pepper,
seeded and chopped

$^1/_2$ pound skinless boneless chicken breasts,
cut into 1-inch pieces

$^1/_2$ teaspoon saffron
threads, crushed

$^3/_4$ cup long-grain white
rice

$1^1/_2$ cups fat-free,
reduced-sodium chicken
broth

$^3/_4$ cup frozen peas

16 mussels, scrubbed and
debearded

$^1/_2$ pound large shrimp,
peeled and deveined

1 Heat a large nonstick skillet over medium-high heat. Add the bacon and cook until beginning to brown, about 3 minutes. Add the garlic, onion, bell peppers, chicken, and saffron. Cook, stirring occasionally, until the vegetables begin to soften, about 2 minutes. Add the rice, broth, and peas and bring to a boil. Cover, reduce the heat to medium-low, and simmer 10 minutes.

2 Add the mussels and shrimp and re-cover the skillet. Raise the heat to medium and simmer until the mussels open and the shrimp are pink and opaque, 8–10 minutes longer. Discard any unopened mussels before serving.

What's for Dinner
 Pair this hearty meal with a refreshing white or green asparagus salad.

COOK'S TIP You'll need a large (at least 12-inch) skillet for this recipe. If it becomes a favorite in your house, you may want to consider purchasing one of the wide, shallow paella pans after which the dish is named. If you don't have saffron on hand, simply omit it from the recipe.

11 *POINTS* per serving

Per serving:
499 Calories • 20 g Total Fat • 7 g Saturated Fat • 135 mg Cholesterol • 691 mg Sodium • 42 mg Total Carbohydrate
4 g Dietary Fiber • 37 g Protein • 78 mg Calcium

Easy Paella

Chicken Fried Rice

In China, fried rice dishes range from simple snacks made from yesterday's leftovers to sumptuous banquets. Fried rice works best when you start with cold, day-old rice, which is drier than freshly cooked rice. Freeze leftover cooked rice to have on hand when the urge for a quick Chinese meal strikes.

*Makes 4 servings
(yields 6 cups)*

2 tablespoons canola oil

2 large eggs, lightly beaten

1 pound skinless boneless chicken breasts, cut into thin strips

1 tablespoon minced peeled fresh ginger

1 garlic clove, minced

1 cup chopped scallions (8–10 scallions)

4 cups cooked long-grain white rice

1½ cups frozen peas and carrots

3 tablespoons reduced-sodium soy sauce

1 teaspoon Asian (dark) sesame oil

 Heat 2 teaspoons of the canola oil in a large nonstick skillet over medium-high heat. Add the eggs and cook, stirring, until firmly scrambled, about 2 minutes. Transfer the eggs to a bowl. Add 1 teaspoon more of the canola oil and the chicken to the skillet. Cook, stirring occasionally, until cooked through, 6–7 minutes; transfer to the bowl with the eggs.

 Add the remaining 1 tablespoon canola oil to the skillet, along with the ginger, garlic, and scallions; cook, stirring, 1 minute. Add the rice and peas and carrots; cook 2 minutes. Stir in the reserved eggs and chicken, the soy sauce, and sesame oil and cook until heated through, 3–5 minutes longer.

What's for Dinner

A heaping bowl of lightly steamed broccoli or spinach complements the fried rice nicely.

10 *POINTS* per serving

Per serving:
488 Calories • 12 g Total Fat • 2 g Saturated Fat • 172 mg Cholesterol • 560 mg Sodium • 54 mg Total Carbohydrate 3 g Dietary Fiber • 37 g Protein • 62 mg Calcium

Greek Chicken Pasta Toss

Roasted sweet peppers, artichoke hearts, and feta cheese give this delicious version of lemon chicken a Mediterranean feel. You could easily substitute another pasta for the short spiral rotini.

*Makes 4 servings
(yield 7 cups)*

1/2 pound rotini

2 tablespoons extra-virgin olive oil

1 pound skinless boneless chicken breasts, cut into thin strips

1/4 teaspoon salt

1/4 teaspoon coarsely ground black pepper

3 garlic cloves, thinly sliced

1 teaspoon dried oregano

1 (7-ounce) jar roasted red peppers, drained and thinly sliced

1 (14-ounce) can artichoke hearts, drained and quartered

1 pint cherry tomatoes, halved

2 tablespoons fresh lemon juice

2 ounces feta cheese, crumbled

2 tablespoons grated Parmesan cheese

1 Bring a large pot of salted water to a boil. Add the rotini and cook according to package directions; drain.

2 Heat 1 tablespoon of the oil in a large nonstick skillet over medium-high heat. Sprinkle the chicken with salt and pepper and add to the skillet. Cook, stirring occasionally, until lightly browned and cooked through, 6–7 minutes.

3 Remove the chicken and add the remaining 1 tablespoon oil to the skillet, along with the garlic and oregano; cook 30 seconds. Add the roasted peppers, artichoke hearts and tomatoes; cook until the tomatoes start to soften, about 3 minutes. Add the lemon juice and the reserved chicken and cook 1 minute longer. Transfer to a large bowl and add the pasta, feta cheese, and Parmesan cheese. Toss well. Serve warm or room temperature.

What's for Dinner

Just serve a simple spinach salad with this hearty pasta.

 COOK'S TIP To make preparation of this quick dish even quicker, start with presliced chicken tenders.

11 *POINTS* per serving

Per serving:
501 Calories • 13 g Total Fat • 4 g Saturated Fat • 80 mg Cholesterol • 750 mg Sodium • 55 mg Total Carbohydrate
3 g Dietary Fiber • 39 g Protein • 144 mg Calcium

DINNER

Cider Chicken with Apples and Thyme

This is a wonderful dish to make when the weather begins to cool and apples are at their peak. Choose a firm apple that will hold its shape while cooking; we call for a Golden Delicious, but a Granny Smith apple would work well, too.

Makes 4 servings

4 (5-ounce) skinless boneless chicken breasts

1/2 teaspoon salt

1/2 teaspoon coarsely ground black pepper

2 teaspoons olive oil

1 cup frozen pearl onions, thawed

4 strips turkey bacon, diced

1 Golden Delicious apple (unpeeled), cored and cut into chunks

1 tablespoon fresh chopped thyme, or 1 teaspoon dried

1 cup apple cider

1/4 cup reduced-sodium chicken broth

Thyme sprigs for garnish

1 Sprinkle the chicken breasts with salt and pepper.

2 Heat the oil in a large nonstick skillet over medium-high heat. Add the chicken and sauté until golden and tender; about 4 minutes on each side; transfer the chicken to a plate.

3 Add the onions and bacon to the skillet. Cook, shaking the pan occasionally, until the onions are softened and browned, about 8 minutes. Add the apple and thyme; cook until the apple is tender and golden, about 5 minutes. Stir in the cider and broth. Raise the heat to high and cook until the sauce boils and thickens slightly, about 5 minutes. Return the chicken to the skillet briefly to heat through. Arrange the chicken on a platter, spoon the sauce on top, and garnish with the thyme sprigs.

What's for Dinner

 Microwaved sweet potato slices, sprinkled with brown sugar and chopped walnuts, is a simple autumn side dish.

 COOK'S TIP For variety, try boneless pork-loin chops or turkey cutlets instead of chicken.

Per serving:
270 Calories • 7 g Total Fat • 1 g Saturated Fat • 92 mg Cholesterol • 617 mg Sodium • 16 mg Total Carbohydrate
2 g Dietary Fiber • 35 g Protein • 67 mg Calcium

6 POINTS per serving

Chinese Grilled Chicken Salad

This chicken salad derives its distinctive taste from Chinese-style barbecue sauce. Look in the Asian aisle of your supermarket, which is also where you will find the sesame oil, soy sauce, and rice vinegar. Rice vinegar is sold in both unseasoned and seasoned varieties; for this recipe, you want seasoned rice vinegar.

Makes 4 servings

1 (1-pound) bag shredded cabbage salad (coleslaw mix)

1 yellow bell pepper, seeded and thinly sliced

4 radishes, thinly sliced

1/2 cup seasoned rice vinegar

1 tablespoon Asian (dark) sesame oil

2 teaspoons reduced-sodium soy sauce

2 teaspoons honey

1 pound thin-sliced skin-less boneless chicken breasts

1/4 cup Chinese-style barbecue sauce

1 Combine the cabbage, bell pepper, and radishes in a large bowl.

2 Whisk together the vinegar, oil, soy sauce, and honey in a small bowl. Pour over the cabbage mixture, toss to coat, and let stand for 10 minutes.

3 Heat a nonstick, ridged grill pan over medium-high heat. Brush both sides of the chicken breasts lightly with the barbecue sauce. Grill until lightly browned, about 3 minutes. Turn and brush with any remaining barbecue sauce. Grill until the chicken is cooked through, about 3 minutes longer. Transfer to a cutting board and let stand 5 minutes before thinly slicing. Serve the chicken over the coleslaw.

What's for Dinner

 This chicken salad is delicious with boiled new red potatoes.

6 POINTS per serving

Per serving:
318 Calories • 7 g Total Fat • 1 g Saturated Fat • 73 mg Cholesterol • 1,377 mg Sodium • 33 mg Total Carbohydrate
4 g Dietary Fiber • 29 g Protein • 78 mg Calcium

Maple-Glazed Chicken

The flavor combination of a zesty spice rub and a sweet maple glaze gives this dish its distinctive appeal. If you prefer, consider grilling the chicken instead of baking it; brush the glaze onto the chicken only once during the last five minutes of grilling to prevent burning.

Makes 4 servings

1 teaspoon paprika

1 teaspoon salt

$1/2$ teaspoon ground cinnamon

$1/2$ teaspoon ground cumin

$1/2$ teaspoon coarsely ground black pepper

4 bone-in chicken breast halves (about $2^1/2$ pounds), skinned

2 tablespoons maple syrup

1 tablespoon butter

1 tablespoon Dijon mustard

1 Preheat the oven to 500°F. Coat a baking sheet with nonstick spray.

2 Combine the paprika, salt, cinnamon, cumin, and pepper in a bowl. Rub the mixture over the chicken breasts and place them on the baking sheet. Position the sheet in the upper one-third of the oven and bake 15 minutes.

3 Meanwhile, combine the maple syrup, butter, and mustard in a small saucepan over low heat. Cook, stirring, until the butter melts and the mixture is well combined.

4 After the chicken has baked for 15 minutes, brush it with the maple glaze and bake 5 minutes. Brush the chicken again and bake until cooked through, about 5 minutes longer.

What's for Dinner

 This chicken pairs superbly with roasted root vegetables.

COOK'S TIP Roasting vegetables in the oven is a snap: Place two sweet potatoes (peeled and cut into ten wedges) and one container Brussels sprouts (washed, trimmed, and halved) in a single layer on a foil lined baking sheet. Drizzle with oil, sprinkle with herbs, and roast in a pre-heated 400°F oven until vegetables are tender and lightly browned, about 30 minutes.

5 *POINTS* per serving

Per serving:
249 Calories • 8 g Total Fat • 3 g Saturated Fat • 105 mg Cholesterol • 719 mg Sodium • 8 mg Total Carbohydrate
1 g Dietary Fiber • 36 g Protein • 38 mg Calcium

Skillet Yellow Rice and Chicken

Known as arroz con pollo, *this dish is a staple of the Latin American diet. Annato, a derivative of achiote seed, traditionally gives the rice its brilliant yellow color. Our version uses more widely available turmeric to achieve a similar hue.*

Makes 4 servings (yield 4 cups)

1 tablespoon olive oil

2 garlic cloves, minced

1/2 cup chopped onion

1/2 cup seeded and chopped green bell pepper

1 pound skinless boneless chicken thighs, cut into 1-inch pieces

1 cup long-grain white rice

1 teaspoon ground turmeric

1 teaspoon ground cumin

2 cups fat-free, reduced-sodium chicken broth

10 pimiento-stuffed green olives, halved crosswise

1 tablespoon capers, drained

1/2 teaspoon salt

1/2 teaspoon coarsely ground black pepper

1/4 cup chopped fresh parsley

Heat the oil in a large nonstick skillet over medium–high heat. Add the garlic, onion, and bell pepper; cook 2 minutes. Add the chicken and cook 2 minutes longer. Stir in the rice, turmeric, and cumin; cook 1 minute. Add the broth, olives, capers, salt, and black pepper; bring to a boil. Cover, reduce the heat, and simmer until the broth has evaporated, about 17 minutes. Remove from the heat and stir in the parsley.

What's for Dinner

A first course of tomato soup starts this meal off in style

COOK'S TIP To shave a few minutes more off the prep time of this quick-fix dish, use 1/4 cup presliced Spanish olives, instead of slicing whole olives yourself.

8 POINTS per serving

Per serving:
375 Calories • 9 g Total Fat • 2 g Saturated Fat • 94 mg Cholesterol • 943 mg Sodium • 42 mg Total Carbohydrate
2 g Dietary Fiber • 28 g Protein • 61 mg Calcium

Chicken Ragoût with Potatoes and Olives

Makes 4 servings

1 teaspoon olive oil

1 1/2 pounds skinless boneless chicken thighs, trimmed of all visible fat

1/2 teaspoon salt

1/4 teaspoon coarsely ground black pepper

1 onion, thinly sliced

1 garlic clove, chopped

3 plum tomatoes, chopped

1 large baking potato, peeled and cubed

10 kalamata olives, pitted and chopped

1/2 cup reduced-sodium chicken broth

1/4 cup dry white wine

1/2 cup chopped fresh basil

The skinless boneless chicken thighs used in this stew are not only full of flavor, but can withstand a longer cooking time than white meat without drying out. Vary the herb to suit your fancy, just be sure to stir it in at the very end of preparation to maximize fresh flavor.

Heat the oil in a large nonstick skillet over medium–high heat. Sprinkle the chicken with the salt and pepper and sauté until browned on both sides, about 5 minutes. Add the onion and garlic; cook until the onion is just tender, about 5 minutes longer. Stir in the tomatoes, potato, olives, broth, and wine. Cover, reduce the heat, and simmer until the chicken is cooked through and the potato tender, about 20 minutes. Remove from the heat and stir in the basil.

What's for Dinner

All you need to round out the meal is steamed broccoli or cauliflower.

 COOK'S TIP To store fresh basil or other fresh herbs, place the stem ends in a glass or jar of cold water; cover the top of the bunch with a plastic food-storage bag and refrigerate.

6 POINTS per serving

Per serving:
306 Calories • 9 g Total Fat • 2 g Saturated Fat • 141 mg Cholesterol • 600 mg Sodium • 19 mg Total Carbohydrate 3 g Dietary Fiber • 36 g Protein • 52 mg Calcium

Kielbasa, Cabbage, and Potato Stew

*Makes 4 servings
(yield 6 cups)*

3/4 pound turkey kielbasa, cut into 3/4-inch pieces

1 (1-pound) head green cabbage, cut into 3/4-inch ribbons

3/4 pound new potatoes, peeled and cut into 1/2-inch chunks

1 onion, sliced

2 carrots, sliced

1 3/4 cups fat-free, reduced-sodium chicken broth

1 cup dry white wine

1 teaspoon caraway seeds

1 bay leaf

1/2 teaspoon dried thyme

Hearty and perfectly suited to cold winter eves, this stew makes a filling one-pot meal. It's a great dish to make ahead, since the cabbage will soften overnight and the smokiness of the kielbasa will infuse the entire dish. Simply cover the stew, refrigerate it, and reheat it when you're ready.

Cook the kielbasa in a large saucepan over medium–high heat until it begins to brown, about 3 minutes. Add the cabbage, potatoes, onion, carrots, broth, wine, caraway seeds, bay leaf, and thyme. Bring to a boil, cover, and cook, stirring occasionally, until the potatoes and cabbage are tender, 15–18 minutes. Discard the bay leaf.

What's for Dinner

This robust stew needs only a light side salad of mixed greens.

5 *POINTS* per serving

Per serving (1 1/2 cups):
255 Calories • 7 g Total Fat • 2 g Saturated Fat • 53 mg Cholesterol • 1,028 mg Sodium • 29 mg Total Carbohydrate
5 g Dietary Fiber • 18 g Protein • 82 mg Calcium

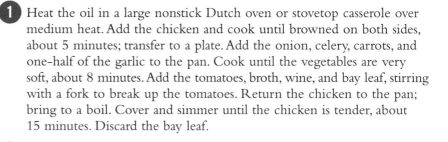

Osso Buco-Style Chicken

This hearty dish contains all the flavors of traditional osso buco made with veal shanks; it even boasts the classic lemon and parsley topping, known as a gremolata. But our chicken version is quicker and easier than traditional osso buco, and it contains a fraction of the fat.

Makes 4 servings

1 teaspoon olive oil

1¹/₂ pounds skinless boneless chicken thighs

¹/₂ cup chopped onion

1 celery stalk, chopped

2 small carrots, chopped

2 large garlic cloves, chopped

1 (14¹/₂-ounce) can whole peeled tomatoes, with their juice

²/₃ cup reduced-sodium chicken broth

¹/₂ cup dry white wine

1 bay leaf

3 tablespoons chopped fresh parsley

1 teaspoon grated lemon zest

 Heat the oil in a large nonstick Dutch oven or stovetop casserole over medium heat. Add the chicken and cook until browned on both sides, about 5 minutes; transfer to a plate. Add the onion, celery, carrots, and one-half of the garlic to the pan. Cook until the vegetables are very soft, about 8 minutes. Add the tomatoes, broth, wine, and bay leaf, stirring with a fork to break up the tomatoes. Return the chicken to the pan; bring to a boil. Cover and simmer until the chicken is tender, about 15 minutes. Discard the bay leaf.

2 Combine the parsley, lemon zest, and the remaining garlic in a small bowl. Sprinkle the mixture over the chicken.

What's for Dinner

 Great with roasted sliced potatoes and steamed green beans.

COOK'S TIP We used chicken thighs for this recipe, but you could also use a cut-up three-pound chicken.

6 *POINTS* per serving

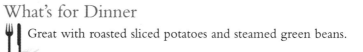

Per serving:
263 Calories • 8 g Total Fat • 2 g Saturated Fat • 141 mg Cholesterol • 543 mg Sodium • 10 mg Total Carbohydrate
2 g Dietary Fiber • 36 g Protein • 69 mg Calcium

Osso Buco-Style Chicken

Stovetop Sausage and Mushroom Casserole

Makes 4 servings
(yield 5 cups)

1/2 pound sweet Italian turkey sausage

2 cups sliced fresh shiitake mushrooms

1 onion, coarsely chopped

1 cup converted white rice

2 cups reduced-sodium chicken broth

2 tablespoons grated Parmesan cheese

1/2 teaspoon coarsely ground black pepper

When the weather outside is chilly, nothing is quite as comforting as a warm casserole. Brimming with sausage, mushrooms, and rice, this recipe lends itself readily to variation; try chopped skinless boneless chicken thighs in place of the turkey sausage. For a more intense mushroom flavor, soak one tablespoon dried porcini mushrooms in hot water for 15 minutes, drain, then add to the saucepan along with the shiitakes.

1 Slice open and remove the casings from the sausage.

2 Spray a large nonstick saucepan with nonstick spray; heat over medium-high heat. Add the sausage, mushrooms, and onion, breaking up the sausage with a fork. Cook until the sausage is browned and the mushrooms and onion are tender, about 8 minutes. Add the rice, stirring to coat, and broth; bring to a boil. Cover, reduce the heat, and simmer until the broth has evaporated and the rice is tender, about 20 minutes. Stir in the Parmesan cheese and pepper.

What's for Dinner

Begin the meal with a salad of peppery watercress and strips of sweet red and yellow bell peppers.

COOK'S TIP Shiitake mushrooms are generally available fresh and widely available dried. If you can't find fresh shiitakes, substitute fresh white or cremini mushrooms and add two tablespoons soaked dried shiitakes.

7 POINTS per serving

Per serving:
321 Calories • 7 g Total Fat • 2 g Saturated Fat • 32 mg Cholesterol • 768 mg Sodium • 48 mg Total Carbohydrate
2 g Dietary Fiber • 17 g Protein • 83 mg Calcium

Stovetop Sausage and Mushroom Casserole

Stuffed Peppers Picadillo

The zesty stuffing in these peppers is a Latin American favorite. Use it to also stuff zucchini, eggplant, acorn squash, or butternut squash.

*Makes 4 servings
(yield 4 cups filling)*

2 large green bell peppers, halved lengthwise and seeded

1/2 pound ground skinless turkey breast

1/2 cup chopped onion

1 garlic clove, minced

1/2 teaspoon ground cumin

1/4 teaspoon ground cinnamon

1 (14 1/2-ounce) can diced tomatoes, with their juice

1 cup quick-cooking rice

1/2 cup water

1/2 cup raisins

5 pimiento-stuffed green olives, chopped

2 tablespoons pine nuts

2 cups marinara sauce

1/4 cup shredded reduced-fat cheddar cheese

1 Preheat the oven to 400°F.

2 Cook the bell peppers in a large pot of boiling water until just tender, about 3 minutes. Rinse under cold running water and drain.

3 Spray a large nonstick skillet with nonstick spray; heat over medium heat. Add the turkey, onion, garlic, cumin, and cinnamon. Cook, breaking up the turkey with a wooden spoon, until no longer pink, about 5 minutes. Stir in the tomatoes, rice, water, raisins, olives, and nuts. Cover and simmer until the rice is tender, about 5 minutes.

4 Spoon the turkey mixture into each pepper. Arrange the peppers in a small baking dish, spoon the marinara sauce over them, and top with the cheese. Bake, uncovered, until the filling is hot and the cheese has melted, about 15 minutes.

What's for Dinner

 Serve the peppers with escarole sautéed with garlic.

9 POINTS per serving

Per serving:
468 Calories • 9 g Total Fat • 2 g Saturated Fat • 38 mg Cholesterol • 1,125 mg Sodium • 75 mg Total Carbohydrate
6 g Dietary Fiber • 24 g Protein • 142 mg Calcium

Sausage and Broccoli Rabe on Mushroom Polenta

Makes 4 servings

1 (1-pound) roll premade wild-mushroom polenta, cut into 12 slices

1 pound broccoli rabe (rapini), trimmed and roughly chopped

1/2 pound sweet Italian turkey sausage

1 cup water

1 tablespoon olive oil

2 garlic cloves, sliced

1/4 teaspoon crushed red pepper

2 tablespoons grated Parmesan cheese

Precooked rolls of polenta, now available in most supermarkets, are quick and easy to use and come in a range of flavors, such as the wild mushroom we use as a base for this dish. Plain or flavored, polenta lends itself readily to so many flavor combinations; keep a roll on hand for a fast weeknight treat.

 Preheat the oven to 400°F. Coat a baking sheet with nonstick spray and arrange the polenta slices in a single layer on the sheet. Spray lightly with the nonstick spray and bake until golden, 10–12 minutes. Remove from the oven and cover to keep warm.

2 Meanwhile, bring a large pot of salted water to a boil. Add the broccoli rabe and cook 2 minutes; drain.

3 Place the sausage in a nonstick skillet; add the 1 cup water and cook over medium–high heat until the water has evaporated and the sausage is browned and cooked through, about 8 minutes. Remove the sausage and cut it into 1/4-inch-thick slices.

4 To the skillet, add the oil, garlic, and crushed red pepper. Cook over medium–high heat, stirring often, until the garlic is lightly golden, about 1 minute. Add the broccoli rabe and cook 2 minutes longer. Return the sausage and cook until heated through, about 1 minute. Transfer the polenta to a serving platter; top with the sausage and broccoli rabe and sprinkle with the Parmesan cheese.

What's for Dinner

 Slices of fresh mozzarella and red and yellow tomatoes make a colorful and flavorful addition to this meal.

5 *POINTS* per serving

Per serving:
241 Calories • 10 g Total Fat • 3 g Saturated Fat • 32 mg Cholesterol • 860 mg Sodium • 23 mg Total Carbohydrate
4 g Dietary Fiber • 15 g Protein • 89 mg Calcium

DINNER

Farfalle Bolognese

Bolognese refers to a hearty "Bologna-style" meat and vegetable sauce. This simple recipe can be made with any combination of lean ground turkey, pork, or beef as an alternative to the veal and chicken. Here we serve it over pretty farfalle (bow tie) pasta.

Makes 4 servings

2 tablespoons olive oil

2 garlic cloves, minced

1/2 cup chopped onion

1 small carrot, chopped

1 teaspoon dried oregano

1/2 pound lean ground veal

1/2 pound ground skinless chicken breast

1 (28-ounce) can whole peeled tomatoes, drained and chopped

1/2 cup red wine

1/4 cup grated Parmesan cheese

1/2 teaspoon salt

1/4 teaspoon coarsely ground black pepper

1/2 pound farfalle

1 Heat the oil in a large nonstick skillet over medium–high heat. Add the garlic, onion, carrot, and oregano; cook, stirring occasionally, until the vegetables begin to soften, about 4 minutes. Add the veal and chicken and cook until no longer pink, about 4 minutes longer. Add the tomatoes and wine and bring to a boil. Reduce the heat and simmer, stirring occasionally, until the sauce begins to thicken, about 15 minutes. Remove from the heat and stir in the Parmesan cheese, salt, and pepper.

2 Meanwhile, bring a large pot of salted water to a boil. Add the farfalle and cook according to package directions; drain. Serve the sauce over the pasta.

What's for Dinner

Serve the Bolognese with a salad of baby greens and a loaf of Italian bread.

COOK'S TIP Prepare a double batch of the meat sauce and freeze half for another time.

10 POINTS per serving

Per serving:
480 Calories • 11 g Total Fat • 3 g Saturated Fat • 84 mg Cholesterol • 777 mg Sodium • 56 mg Total Carbohydrate
5 g Dietary Fiber • 36 g Protein • 178 mg Calcium

Farfalle Bolognese

DINNER

Beef Fajitas with Mango Salsa

The easy tropical salsa served with these flavorful fajitas can double as a great low-fat dip when served with baked tortilla chips or as a topping for a quesadilla. It also makes a zippy accompaniment for grilled or broiled fish, chicken, or pork, turning dinner into a fiesta.

**Makes 4 servings
(yield 1¹/₃ cups salsa)**

1 mango, chopped

1 plum tomato, chopped

2 tablespoons finely chopped red onion + 1 cup thinly sliced

1 tablespoon chopped cilantro

1 teaspoon salt

2 tablespoons fresh lime juice

1 pound flank steak, cut into thin strips

2 teaspoons chili powder

1 teaspoon ground coriander

¹/₂ teaspoon dried oregano

2 teaspoons canola oil

1 green bell pepper, seeded and thinly sliced

1 jalapeño pepper, seeded and thinly sliced (wear gloves to prevent irritation)

2 teaspoons Worcestershire sauce

1 tomato, cut into 8 wedges

4 reduced-fat burrito-size flour tortillas, warmed

 Combine the mango, tomato, chopped onion, cilantro, ¹/₄ teaspoon of the salt, and 1 tablespoon of the lime juice in a bowl; toss to mix and set the salsa aside.

2 Combine the steak, chili powder, coriander, and oregano in another bowl; turn to coat the meat. Heat the oil in a large nonstick skillet over medium-high heat. Add the steak, sliced onion, bell pepper, jalapeño pepper, Worcestershire sauce, and the remaining ³/₄ teaspoon salt. Cook, stirring occasionally, 6 minutes. Add the tomato wedges and cook until the steak is done to taste, about 1 minute longer for medium-rare. Remove from the heat and stir in the remaining 1 tablespoon lime juice.

3 Mound one-quarter of the beef mixture in a strip down the center of each tortilla, leaving a 1¹/₂-inch border at either end. Fold the bottom flap up over the filling then roll the sides in to form a cone. Serve with the salsa on the side.

What's for Dinner

 In traditional Mexican style, complete the meal with a side of rice and beans.

COOK'S TIP If you make the mango salsa to serve as a dip, add one-quarter teaspoon crushed red pepper to make it spicy.

8 POINTS per serving

Per serving:
399 Calories • 12 g Total Fat • 4 g Saturated Fat • 46 mg Cholesterol • 1,051 mg Sodium • 44 mg Total Carbohydrate
13 g Dietary Fiber • 31 g Protein • 65 mg Calcium

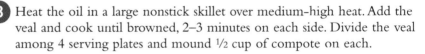

Veal Scaloppine with Cranberry-Fig Compote

Makes 4 servings
(yield 2 cups compote)

1 cup dry white wine

1/2 cup water

1/2 pound dried figs, chopped

1/2 cup dried cranberries

1 tablespoon sugar

1/4 teaspoon almond extract

3/4 teaspoon salt

2 tablespoons all-purpose flour

1 teaspoon garlic powder

1/4 teaspoon ground nutmeg

1/4 teaspoon coarsely ground black pepper

1 pound veal scaloppine (from top round leg)

1 tablespoon canola oil

The dried fruit compote that we use to finish this simple and scrumptious dish also makes an excellent accompaniment to pork or poultry. For rave reviews from your family, try it on Thanksgiving in place of the traditional cranberry sauce.

 1 Combine the wine, water, figs, cranberries, sugar, almond extract, and 1/4 teaspoon of the salt in a saucepan and bring to a boil. Reduce the heat and simmer, stirring occasionally, until thickened, about 15 minutes; remove from the heat.

2 Combine the flour, garlic powder, nutmeg, the remaining 1/2 teaspoon salt, and the pepper in a shallow bowl. Dip the veal in the flour mixture to coat.

3 Heat the oil in a large nonstick skillet over medium-high heat. Add the veal and cook until browned, 2–3 minutes on each side. Divide the veal among 4 serving plates and mound 1/2 cup of compote on each.

What's for Dinner

 Serve the veal with steamed spinach and roasted potato wedges.

COOK'S TIP To roast potato wedges, scrub two baking potatoes and cut each into eight wedges. Arrange in one layer in a baking tray. Drizzle the potatoes with one teaspoon extra-virgin olive oil, sprinkle with salt and pepper, and roast in a preheated 375°F oven until cooked and browned, about 30 minutes.

Per serving:
395 Calories • 7 g Total Fat • 1 g Saturated Fat • 88 mg Cholesterol • 506 mg Sodium • 57 mg Total Carbohydrate 8 g Dietary Fiber • 27 g Protein • 92 mg Calcium

 8 POINTS per serving

DINNER

Lamb Kebabs with Minted Couscous Salad

*Makes 6 servings
(yield 8 cups salad)*

2 (5-ounce) boxes Israeli couscous

4$^{1}/_{2}$ cups water

2 tomatoes, seeded and chopped

1 cucumber, peeled, halved lengthwise, seeded, and sliced

$^{1}/_{2}$ cup thinly sliced red onion

$^{1}/_{4}$ cup chopped fresh mint

1 tablespoon grated lemon zest

1 tablespoon fresh lemon juice

1 tablespoon + 2 teaspoons extra-virgin olive oil

1 tablespoon cider vinegar

$^{1}/_{4}$ pound feta cheese, crumbled

1 teaspoon salt

1 teaspoon coarsely ground black pepper

1 pound boneless lean lamb, trimmed of all visible fat and cut into 1-inch cubes

1 teaspoon dried oregano

Couscous comes in two varieties—the familiar small granular type, and a larger pearl-shaped type (about the same size as pearl barley) known as Israeli or Mediterranean couscous. The main ingredient of this colorful salad is Israeli couscous. It is packaged in boxes of about five ounces; if you buy a brand that has a flavor packet inside, do not use the seasonings to make this recipe.

1 Preheat the broiler.

2 Combine the couscous and water in a saucepan; bring to a boil. Cover, reduce the heat, and simmer until tender, about 15 minutes. Rinse the couscous under cold running water, drain well, and transfer to a large bowl. Stir in the tomatoes, cucumber, onion, mint, lemon zest, lemon juice, 1 tablespoon of the oil, the vinegar, feta cheese, $^{1}/_{2}$ teaspoon of the salt, and $^{1}/_{2}$ teaspoon of the pepper.

3 Combine the lamb, the remaining 2 teaspoons oil, the oregano, the remaining $^{1}/_{2}$ teaspoon salt, and the remaining $^{1}/_{2}$ teaspoon pepper in another bowl, tossing to coat the meat. Thread the lamb onto 6 metal skewers. Broil the kebabs, 5 inches from the heat, until the lamb is just cooked through, about 8 minutes, turning once. Spoon the couscous onto a platter and top with the kebabs.

What's for Dinner

Serve with steamed asparagus spears.

 COOK'S TIP If you can't find Israeli couscous, use one 10-ounce box of plain granular couscous.

8 POINTS per serving

Per serving:
388 Calories • 12 g Total Fat • 5 g Saturated Fat • 68 mg Cholesterol • 650 mg Sodium • 42 mg Total Carbohydrate • 4 g Dietary Fiber • 26 g Protein • 138 mg Calcium

Savory Lamb Stew

Brimming with pearl onions, potato cubes, and peas, as well as scrumptious chunks of lamb, this dish is an ideal Sunday supper. Use boneless lamb shoulder meat that you or your butcher cut into cubes—it will be leaner than packaged, precut stew meat.

Makes 4 servings
(yield 7 cups)

2 tablespoons all-purpose flour

1/2 teaspoon salt

1/2 teaspoon coarsely ground black pepper

1 1/4 pounds lamb stew meat (preferably boneless lamb shoulder, trimmed of all visible fat and cut into 1-inch cubes)

2 teaspoons olive oil

1 (9-ounce) package frozen pearl onions, thawed

1 tablespoon tomato paste

1 medium baking potato, peeled and cubed

1 cup baby carrots

2 cups reduced-sodium chicken broth

1 cup frozen peas, thawed

2 tablespoons chopped fresh parsley

 Combine the flour, salt, and pepper in a large plastic storage bag. Add the lamb, seal tightly, and shake to coat.

Heat the oil is a large nonstick saucepan over medium-high heat. Add the lamb and cook until browned all over, about 5 minutes. Add the onions and tomato paste, stirring to coat well. Add the potato, carrots, and broth; bring to a boil. Cover, reduce the heat, and simmer until the lamb and vegetables are tender, about 20 minutes. Stir in the peas and parsley and continue to cook briefly to heat through.

What's for Dinner

Serve this down-home stew over a bed of egg noodles or rice.

7 POINTS per serving

Per serving (1 3/4 cups):
326 Calories • 10 g Total Fat • 3 g Saturated Fat • 88 mg Cholesterol • 727 mg Sodium • 26 mg Total Carbohydrate
5 g Dietary Fiber • 33 g Protein • 98 mg Calcium

225

Pork Cutlets Cordon Bleu

This quick and easy work-night version of the classic French dish lets you make a special dinner in minutes. Although we have retained the traditional ham and cheese topping, these cutlets, unlike the original recipe, are not breaded and cook in a speedy ten minutes.

Makes 4 servings

1¼ pounds pork tenderloin

½ teaspoon salt

½ teaspoon coarsely ground black pepper

2 tablespoons all-purpose flour

1 teaspoon olive oil

4 (1-ounce) slices reduced-fat deli Swiss cheese, halved

4 (1-ounce) slices reduced-fat deli ham, halved

¼ cup dry white wine

¼ cup reduced-sodium chicken broth

1 tablespoon chopped fresh sage, or 1 teaspoon dried

1 Cut the pork diagonally across the grain into eight ¼-inch-thick cutlets. Place the cutlets between sheets of wax paper and pound to a thickness of ⅛ inch. Season both sides of each cutlet with the salt and pepper. Sprinkle the flour onto a sheet of wax paper or a plate; lightly dredge the cutlets in the flour, shaking off excess.

2 Heat the oil in a large nonstick skillet over medium-high heat. Sauté the pork 3 minutes; turn the cutlets over and top each with a slice of ham and a slice of cheese. Add the wine and broth; bring to a boil. Boil, until the liquid is reduced by half, about 3 minutes. Sprinkle with sage. Transfer the cutlets to a platter and spoon the sauce on top.

What's for Dinner

 Serve with parslied rice and baked apples.

COOK'S TIP If you prefer, substitute an equal amount of water for the white wine.

7 POINTS per serving

Per serving:
323 Calories • 12 g Total Fat • 5 g Saturated Fat • 115 mg Cholesterol • 696 mg Sodium • 5 mg Total Carbohydrate
0 g Dietary Fiber • 44 g Protein • 329 mg Calcium

Apricot-Glazed Pork Skewers with Mango Quinoa

Tropical and tantalizing, this is a perfect summer meal—satisfying but not heavy, fruity but not sweet. Look for a mango with a speckled reddish-yellow hue that yields slightly to pressure. A sprinkling of chopped scallion makes an eye-pleasing finishing touch for this creative dish.

Makes 6 servings
(yield 4 1/2 cups quinoa)

1 cup quinoa, rinsed well under warm running water and drained

2 cups water

2 tablespoons fresh lime juice

1 tablespoon orange juice

1 tablespoon cider vinegar

1 tablespoon extra-virgin olive oil

3/4 teaspoon salt

1 ripe mango, peeled and cut into 1/2-inch cubes

4 scallions, chopped

1/4 cup finely chopped red onion

1/4 cup raisins

1/4 cup walnuts, toasted and coarsely chopped

1/2 cup apricot preserves

3 tablespoons Dijon mustard

1 shallot, finely chopped

1 teaspoon reduced-sodium soy sauce

1 1/2 pounds pork tenderloin

1/2 teaspoon coarsely ground black pepper

1 Combine the quinoa and water in a saucepan; bring to a boil. Cover, reduce the heat, and simmer until the water has been absorbed, about 10 minutes. Transfer to a large bowl and let cool slightly.

2 Whisk together the lime juice, orange juice, vinegar, oil, and 1/4 teaspoon of the salt. Add the mixture to the bowl with the quinoa, along with the mango, scallions, onion, raisins, and walnuts; toss to coat.

3 Preheat the broiler.

4 Whisk together the preserves, mustard, shallot, and soy sauce in a small bowl. Thinly slice the pork on the diagonal across the grain. Sprinkle the slices with the pepper and the remaining 1/2 teaspoon salt and thread onto 12 long metal skewers. Place the skewers on the rack of a broiler pan and brush with the glaze. Broil, 7 inches from the heat, until the glaze begins to caramelize, about 8 minutes, turning the skewers once and brushing occasionally with the glaze. Bring any remaining glaze to a boil in a small saucepan, boil 1 minute, and spoon over the kebabs. Serve with the quinoa.

What's for Dinner

Steamed sugar snap peas add a refreshing crunch to the pork and quinoa.

10 POINTS per serving

Per serving (with 3/4 cup quinoa):
460 Calories • 14g Total Fat • 3 g Saturated Fat • 78 mg Cholesterol • 429 mg Sodium • 53 mg Total Carbohydrate 4 g Dietary Fiber • 32 g Protein • 71 mg Calcium

227

Herb-Crusted Pork Tenderloin with Red Onion Jam

Searing meat in a skillet before roasting, as we do here with the pork tenderloin, helps create a crusty exterior and locks in the juices. Cooking the onions slowly over low heat releases all their natural sweetness, making a melt-in-your-mouth topping for the meat.

Makes 4 servings

1 tablespoon butter

3 red onions (about 1 1/2 pounds), thinly sliced

2 teaspoons sugar

1 teaspoon salt

1/4 cup water

1 pound pork tenderloin

1/2 teaspoon coarsely ground black pepper

1 tablespoon chopped fresh rosemary

1 garlic clove, minced

2 teaspoons olive oil

1 Preheat the oven to 475°F.

2 Heat the butter in a large skillet over low heat until melted. Add the onions, sugar, 1/2 teaspoon of the salt, and the water; bring to a boil. Cover and simmer until the water has evaporated and the onions are fork-tender, about 20 minutes. Remove from the heat and keep warm.

3 Sprinkle the pork with the pepper and the remaining 1/2 teaspoon salt. Spray a nonstick skillet with nonstick spray. Add the pork and brown on both sides, about 5 minutes. Transfer to a small roasting pan.

4 Meanwhile, combine the rosemary, garlic, and oil in a small bowl. Rub the mixture over the tenderloin. Roast until the pork reaches an internal temperature of 160°F, 10–15 minutes. Let stand 10 minutes before slicing into 1-inch slices. Spoon the onion jam over the pork.

What's for Dinner

 Mashed potatoes and applesauce round this meal out well.

5 POINTS per serving

Per serving:
263 Calories • 10 g Total Fat • 4 g Saturated Fat • 75 mg Cholesterol • 665 mg Sodium • 17 mg Total Carbohydrate
3 g Dietary Fiber • 26 g Protein • 45 mg Calcium

Metric Conversion Chart

If you are converting the recipes in this book to metric measurements, use the following chart as a guide.

Teaspoons	Tablespoons	Cups	Fluid Ounces	Volume	
3 teaspoons	1 tablespoon		1/2 fluid ounce	1/4 teaspoon	1 milliliter
6 teaspoons	2 tablespoons	1/8 cup	1 fluid ounce	1/2 teaspoon	2 milliliters
8 teaspoons	2 tablespoons plus 2 teaspoons	1/6 cup		1 teaspoon	5 milliliters
12 teaspoons	4 tablespoons	1/4 cup	2 fluid ounces	1 tablespoon	15 milliliters
15 teaspoons	5 tablespoons minus 1 teaspoon	1/3 cup		2 tablespoons	30 milliliters
16 teaspoons	5 tablespoons plus 1 teaspoon	1/3 cup		3 tablespoons	45 milliliters
18 teaspoons	6 tablespoons	1/4 cup plus 2 tablespoons	3 fluid ounces	1/4 cup	60 milliliters
24 teaspoons	8 tablespoons	1/2 cup	4 fluid ounces	1/3 cup	75 milliliters
30 teaspoons	10 tablespoons	1/2 cup plus 2 tablespoons	5 fluid ounces	1/2 cup	125 milliliters
32 teaspoons	10 tablespoons	2/3 cup plus 2 teaspoons		2/3 cup	150 milliliters
36 teaspoons	12 tablespoons	3/4 cup	6 fluid ounces	3/4 cup	175 milliliters
42 teaspoons	14 tablespoons	1 cup minus 2 tablespoons	7 fluid ounces	1 cup	225 milliliters
45 teaspoons	15 tablespoons	1 cup minus 2 tablespoons		1 quart	1 liter
48 teaspoons	16 tablespoons	1 cup	8 fluid ounces		

Note: Measurement of less than 1/8 teaspoons is considered a dash or a pinch.

Weight		Length		Oven Temperature			
1 ounce	30 grams	1 inch	25 millimeters	250°F	120°C	400°F	200°C
1/4 pound	120 grams	1 inch	2.5 centimeters	275°F	140°C	425°F	220°C
1/2 pound	240 grams			300°F	150°C	450°F	230°C
3/4 pound	360 grams			325°F	160°C	475°F	250°C
1 pound	480 grams			350°F	180°C	500°F	260°C
				375°F	190°C	525°F	270°C

Index

Page references in *italics* refer to photographs.